IT'S NOT THE END OF THE WORLD!

BUT IT'S LATER THAN YOU THINK.

Looking into the future by looking into the Bible

BILLIE GORHAM

ISBN: 978-1-54391-604-1 (print)
ISBN: 978-1-54391-605-8 (ebook)

THE RUSSIANS ARE COMING!

The Bear Awakens!

What has the Russian bear got to do with prophecy?

The prophet, Ezekiel, tells us that after Israel becomes a nation and is brought back to the mountains of Zion, and is dwelling ***in safety***, that a coalition of forces, from the far north, from the Middle East, and Africa will descend on Israel to take a spoil. They definitely are not dwelling in safety now, but watch for a peace treaty between Israel and the Arabs that surround her and she will let down her defenses with a false sense of peace. Then, I believe, Russia will attack.

Ezekiel 38: 14 "...say unto Gog, Thus says the Lord God; In that day..... you shall come from your place out of the far north, you and many people with you.....against my people of Israel." Russia is to the far north of Israel and has as its allies Iran, Syria, Turkey, Libya and Ethiopia. Russia is taking over the countries around Israel, and making military moves to the countries in the Middle East as well as to the north and around the Arctic Circle. So, let's look at Ezekiel to know what is going on with Russia.

Ezekiel 38:2 "Son of man, set your face against Gog, the land of Magog, the chief prince of Meschech and Tubal, and prophesy against him.

Gog is probably a title like czar or pharaoh, a leader who will arise in the land of Magog, in the "remote parts of the north." Magog was a son of Japheth, who was a son of Noah. He founded those that were named

Magogites. They lived in the areas now known as Russia, the former Soviet republics, and central Asia. Russia extends across the "remote parts of the north."

Ezekiel 38: 5 "You will come from your place in the far north with Persia, (Iran,) *Cush,* (Sudan,) *Put (* Algeria, Tunisia), *Gomer, (*Turkey,) *Beth Togarmah, (*Turkey, Armenia,*) from the far north, Ethiopia, and Libya with them; all of them with shield and helmet: 6 Gomer, and all his troops; the house of Togarmah of the north quarters, and all his troops and many people with you."* (Who are the "many people with you"? Possibly they are additional Islamic allies. One in seven Russian citizens, about 20 million people, are Muslims.)

The bear has been pretending to sleep but is now letting the world know it is awake and moving, as can be seen by the following headlines.

Headline: ***"Russia Flexing Its Muscles;"***

The Russian government is indeed flexing its muscles and watching to see who blinks first. From moving more tanks into Ukraine, to transferring nuclear weapons-capable units to Crimea, to announcing that it will start flying long-range bombers over the Gulf of Mexico, the Kremlin is determined to be the leader in global affairs. The invasion of Crimea should have been the wake-up call.

2014 Headline: ***" Russia invades Crimea, instigates civil war in Ukraine;"***

4 June 2015: "Ukraine's Poroshenko warns of 'full-scale' Russia invasion"

(Through Ukraine and the Black Sea is the most direct route to Israel.)

The Russian invasion of Ukraine has many precedents, from the attempt to take over Afghanistan in 1979 to the aggression in Georgia in 2008. On those invasions, as in Ukraine, they used Russian insurgents to instigate war. Another country close to Ukraine, Serbia, is welcoming Putin and his elite Russian troops, to train with the Serbian army. All of these countries are paths to the Middle East.

As early as 1982, the Israeli Defense Forces had uncovered a secret but massive cache of Soviet weaponry in tunnels in Lebanon, for the launching of a full-scale invasion of Israel and the oil-rich nations of the Middle East. (Russia has one of her ships in the Mediterranean Sea today.) At the same time, Iran's Ahmadinejad was saying "Wipe Israel off the map."

President Obama, when he was in office, was supposedly considering giving Ukraine military support and lethal aid as required by the Ukraine Freedom Support Act. But the former Soviet leader Mikhail Gorbachev warned that World War III and a major nuclear war could start over the Ukrainian war.

2015 Predictions: World War 3 Could Be Inevitable As Russia Leads World Into New Kind of Conflict November 25,2015 By Vladimir Isachenkov, Associated Press

Using Russia's air cover, Iran and Hezbollah pour in fighters to central, northern Syria

Posted: Wednesday, October 14, 2015 9:35 am | *Updated: 10:00 am, Wed Oct 14, 2015.*

Syria, Israel's neighbor to the north, has invited Russia to help them destroy rebel strongholds. As a result of years of fighting with the government and Islamic terrorists, Muslim refugees have poured into Europe, Turkey and other countries around the world, including the U.S. It is an open conduit for terrorists to enter and attack any nation.

Headline: Vladimir Putin Sets Stage For World War 3, Expands Russia's Nuclear Weapons Defenses Near Europe

"Setting the stage for World War III , Russian leader, Vladimir Putin, is threatening to expand Russia's nuclear weapons defense systems near Europe in response to efforts by NATO and the United States to extend air and anti-missile defense coverage over Europe. It is also threatening to expand its nuclear missile defense systems in cooperation with the BRICS nations, Brazil, Russia, India, China, and South Africa as part of joint defense projects. This past fall, the number of Russian nuclear weapons surpassed the United States for the first time in 40 years".

The Russian Defense Minister Sergei Shoigu said long-range bombers would begin conducting flights along Russian borders and over the Arctic Ocean. He added, 'In the current situation we have to maintain military presence in the western Atlantic and eastern Pacific, as well as the Caribbean and the Gulf of Mexico.'"

Never in the last 2500 years have Russia and Iran had a military alliance, but headlines in 2005 read **"IRAN REGARDS RUSSIA AS POSSIBLE PARTNER TO BUILD 20 NUCLEAR POWER PLANTS" and "KREMLIN READY TO DEFEND IRAN."** And between 1992 and 2000, Russian arms sales to Iran topped $4 billion. Then, the headline: ***"IRAN DEVELOPS NUCLEAR ARMS."*** To complete the picture, a headline on Feb. 17, 2005, read: **"LIBYA AND ALGERIA READY TO BUY RUSSIAN ARMS IF RUSSIA WRITES OFF DEBTS"**

Ezekiel 38:11 And you shall say, I will go up to the land of unwalled villages; I will go to them that are at rest, that dwell safely, (Will they be dwelling safely because a peace treaty has finally been made?) *all of them dwelling without walls, and having neither bars nor gates, 12 to the people who dwell in **the center of the world**.* (The Middle East is called the cradle of civilization and thus the center of the world.*) 15 "And you shall come from your place out of the far north, you, and many people with you, all of them riding upon horses, a great company, and a mighty army."*

(They will come on horses with burnable weaponry and that doesn't make sense because in this modern age, they would come on airplanes, and tanks and ships, right? So, what happens to make everything turn back to a former way of life?

Perhaps a nuclear attack on the electric grid or a sunblast that hits it?)

An EMP (electromagnetic pulse) can be caused by a high-altitude nuclear device that will interact with the Earth's atmosphere,

ionosphere, and magnetic field to produce an EMP radiating down to the Earth and create electrical currents in the Earth.

Headline: "'Extreme solar storm' could have pulled the plug on Earth"

"Satellites, power and water supplies would have been hit if a billion-ton plasma cloud had erupted from the sun a week earlier. The date of 23, July, 2012, could have been the day the lights went out, along with suddenly not-so-smart phones, computers, satellite transmissions, GPS navigation systems, televisions, radio broadcasts, hospital equipment, electric pumps and water supplies."

Headline: "Russian army orders horses for paratrooper division."

39:1 Therefore, son of man, prophesy against Gog, and say, Thus says the Lord God; Behold, I am against you, O Gog, chief prince of Meshech and Tubal; 2 And I will turn you around and leave but the sixth part of you, and will cause you ***to come up from the far north parts, and will bring you upon the mountains of Israel.***

Question: What is the rest of the world doing?

Sheba, Dedan and Merchants of Tarshish will ask, "Are you come to take a spoil?" The nations not involved will ask them why they are invading Israel, but will not try or be able to stop them.

Question: Why are they coming?

Russian leader and ally of Putin, Vladimir Zhirinovsky, wrote a book about expanding the Russian empire to the south using the code-name, "Final Thrust to the South." In it, he said, "Russia reaching the shores of the Indian Ocean and the Mediterranean Sea is a task that will be the salvation of the Russian nation….Russia will grow rich."

Ezekiel 39:12 says. "To take a spoil and to take a prey; to turn your hand upon the ***desolate*** *places that are now inhabited, and upon the people that are gathered out of the nations, which have gotten cattle and goods, that dwell in the midst of the land."*

Headline in 2004: ***"ISRAEL STRIKES BLACK GOLD"***

In *Deuteronomy 33:13,15,16,19,24,* Moses spoke of treasures under the deep, precious things of the hill, precious things of the earth, treasures hid in the sand, and dipping his foot in oil. He said, *"Their land will yield the precious fruits of the deep lying beneath the ancient mountains."*

But Russia and her allies don't just want to control all of the oil, they want to control all of the seas through which the oil is transported, essentially controlling any and every country that depends on oil.

Question: What will happen?

When Russia and her allies, Iran, Libya, Turkey, etc. get to the mountains around Israel, God is going to annihilate them in a great storm of fury with an earthquake, lightning, floods, burning sulfur, and hail stones. It will look like nuclear warfare on steroids. Then there will be fires in Magog and on the coastlands.

Ezekiel 38:19-22 "Surely in that day there shall be a great earthquake in the land of Israel, ...and the mountains shall be thrown down, and the steep places shall fall, and every wall shall fall to the ground.....and every man's sword shall be against his brother. And I will bring judgment to him with pestilence and with bloodshed; and I will rain upon him, ... with flooding, great hailstones, fire, and burning sulphur, ...and will send fire on Magog and coastlands."......

Ezekiel 39:9 "They that dwell in the cities of Israel shall ....set on fire and burn the weapons...and they shall make fires with them for seven years..."

Because Israel will be burning weapons as fuel for seven years, this cannot be the battle of Armageddon, since immediately after Armageddon, the Lord comes to defeat the armies and begin the Millennium rule of Christ.

Ezekiel 39:11 "And it shall come to pass in that day, that I will give to Gog a burial place there of graves in Israel,.....they shall call it the valley of

Hamon-gog. 12 And seven months shall the house of Israel be burying them, that they may cleanse the land."

At the Battle of Armageddon, there will be no burying because there will be too many to bury. But, at this time, with earthquakes, warfare, etc. the Dome of the Rock may disappear and the Third Jewish Temple will be re-built.

39:1 Therefore, son of man, prophesy against Gog, and say, Thus says the Lord God; Behold, I am against you, O Gog, chief prince of Meshech and Tubal; 2 And I will turn you around and leave but the sixth part of you, and will cause you to come up from the far north parts, and will bring you upon the mountains of Israel.

Headline: ***Nuclear War Over Turkey Shooting Down Plane*** By Polina Tikhonova on November 25, 2015 in Politics, Russia

Russia is now bombing Syrian targets, supposedly ISIS, but it looks as if they are bombing U.S. supported rebels. Syria is next door to Israel. But the outcome of this Russian attack on Israel was foretold by the prophets.

Joel 2:20 But I will remove far off from you the northern army, and will drive him into a land barren and desolate, with his face toward the east sea, and his back toward the western sea, and his stink shall come up, and his foul odor shall come up, because he has done monstrous things.

Suddenly everything changes for Israel and its people when they see what God does to the invading armies of Russia and her allies.

Introduction

Everyone is feeling it, this unidentifiable awareness that something is about to happen that will change the world. Those who don't mention it either have tuned out or are completely ignorant of current events. It's like we are all holding our breath anticipating when the next tragedy will occur.

2 Timothy 3:1 This know also, that in the last days perilous (DANGEROUS) times shall come.

We've put the tragedy of 9/11 behind us because it was sixteen years ago and the fear of a variety of calamities are moving through our nightly news so quickly, we cannot pay attention to one before another one pops up. Between droughts, fires, earthquakes, tornados and hurricanes, terrorists on every continent bombing and beheading, countries threatening nuclear war, and a civil war threatening America, fear is everywhere and the future looks hopeless. What is going on? What is going to happen next?

Returning from a trip to South Africa, I sat down in the crowded airplane beside a huge man who overlapped both of our seats and who looked at me with a frown and growled, "I do not talk on airplanes!" That was great with me because I was looking forward to reading a book on prophecy that I had recently purchased.

When he saw the title of the book, he asked, "You don't believe all that nonsense, do you?"

I replied that indeed I did believe it and he started in talking non-stop for eight hours across the Atlantic Ocean, telling me why I should not believe in God, the Bible and the prophecies that are in it. At the end, he finally allowed me to tell him some of the reasons that I know God is real and that the Bible is true. He agreed to consider what I had said and admitted that he had never heard about experiences like that before.

When I mention Bible prophecy, and I mention prophecy a lot because I really believe that we are in the last of the last days, people are quick to point out that we have been waiting for two thousand years for the return of Jesus and things are just like they have always been. The Bible even tells us that people will say that very thing: "It's always been like this."

2 Peter 3:3 Knowing this first, that there shall come in the last days scoffers, walking after their own lusts, 4 and saying, Where is the promise of his coming? For since the fathers fell asleep, all things continue as they were from the beginning of the creation.

Jude 18 How that they told you there should be mockers in the last time, who should walk after their own ungodly lusts. 19 These are they who cause divisions, worldly, having not the Spirit.

2 Peter 3:8 But, beloved, be not ignorant of this one thing, that one day is with the Lord as a thousand years, and a thousand years as one day. 9 The Lord is not slack concerning his promise, as some men count slackness: but is long –suffering toward us, not willing that any should perish, but that all should come to repentance.

2 Peter 3:10 But the day of the Lord will come as a thief in the night; in the which the heavens shall pass away with a great noise, and the elements shall melt with fervent heat, the earth also and the works that are therein shall be burned up.

First of all, I don't want to think about End Times any more than you do. It just seems to be rather relevant these days. I should never have read "The Late Great Planet Earth" when I was a teen-ager. Then maybe I would not have become so interested in Bible prophecy. That would have been fine with my children because they think they have earned extra crowns just having to listen to me all these years. I should have buried my head in the sand like a lot of other people; then I would not have to be constantly comparing the evening news with what the Bible says.

I cannot help it. All of the signs are there and it just seems too indifferent to let people run over a cliff because they cannot comprehend the warnings. It is like a really fast train approaching and we are all sitting in the middle of the tracks talking about things that don't matter when we ought to be trying to get to the other side.

CONTENTS

CHAPTER 1

So, What Time Is It?

An Overview

Daniel 12:4 ..."Seal the book, even to the time of the end: many shall run to and fro, and knowledge shall be increased." Nahum 2:4 "The chariots shall rage in the streets, they shall jostle one against another in the broad ways: they shall seem like torches, they shall run like lightning."

If you are asking yourself every evening after watching the news, "What is happening to our world?" you haven't seen anything yet!

But you can find comfort in the fact that God is in control. He told us in His word exactly what would happen and gave us sign posts for the road ahead. These are some of the signs to look for to find out where we are and where we are going:

1. ISRAEL RETURNS

People will say that everyone has talked about the end of the age and the return of Christ for thousands of years and that is true. The disciples talked about it. First century Church leaders spoke about it. Even Christopher Columbus was expecting it.

But the difference in what people have said for years is that Israel is now a nation (1948), and they are back in their land as one nation, with one head of state. The desert is blooming like a rose and there are homes and gardens in Israel where there was only desolation before, just as the Bible prophesied.

2. PERSECUTION OF CHRISTIANS

If you have not noticed the courts destroying the rights of Christians, you have been in your own zoned-out state. People have been threatened, persecuted, and prosecuted for praying, for witnessing, for carrying their Bibles, and for talking about Jesus in the workplace and in the schools. In China, the Muslim world, parts of Africa and South America, there has always been extreme persecution and people are being martyred every day.

3. EARTHQUAKES, HURRICANES, OTHER NATURAL DISASTERS

But God knows what is happening. He knows exactly what is going to happen next. His Word tells us what has been and what will be. It says "earthquakes in different places." I thought I understood the Lord to tell me a few years ago that there would be an earthquake right through the middle of the U.S. I thought that was my imagination because everyone knows that earthquakes happen near oceans, right? Then I found out about an earthquake that had displaced part of the Mississippi River in the 1800's, the New Madrid Fault. Not only could it happen again, scientists are expecting it. It is also interesting how many earthquake tremors are being felt in Oklahoma and Texas.

4. WARS

It says that there will constantly be wars and rumors of wars. There have always been wars. Does the fact that it is happening on world-wide scales mean anything? I have given you an overview of what the Bible says is coming. But in Revelation, Daniel, Ezekiel, and the other prophets, it give us very specific details of what has happened, what is happening, and what will happen. It is the most exciting time to be alive, because any day, the Lord may say, "Come up hither."

5. GOSPEL PREACHED AROUND THE WORLD

There is also the fact that via television and satellite, the gospel is being preached throughout the world. Jesus said that it would happen right before His second coming.

6. ALL-SEEING GOVERNMENT

There is a computer already built that can number every human on the planet. It can do one thousand TRILLION calculations per SECOND. Just recently, a law has been passed allowing the government to examine any and every communication, from your cell phones to your e-mails, from your land lines to your television programs.

"Project Echelon" can produce information on every one of the 600-700 billion people on earth **every second**. If you see what is posted on social media, it appears that people do not want privacy anyway.

These are just previews of coming attractions. Look for these signs next:

1. A PEACE TREATY BETWEEN ISRAEL AND ARABS

2. A RUSSIAN INVASION

When the wall was taken down between Russia and the rest of the world, we thought that we would now have peace. The Communists had another strategy and Russia is getting ready to rumble again. Ezekiel 38 told us this would happen. They and their allies will go toward Israel to "take a spoil." Oil has been found underneath Israel and I believe that Russian armies will come through Ukraine, Turkey, and Syria to attack Israel. Ukraine is having a hard time keeping Russia from taking over again and other countries around Russia are getting nervous. They already have their planes in Syria. But God will destroy Russia and her allies when they come to attack Israel.

3. A SPIRITUAL REVIVAL IN ISRAEL

Because of this miracle, Israel will believe in Jesus as the Messiah and 144,000 Messianic Jews will begin preaching.

4. THE TEMPLE REBUILT

There will be a temple built again in Jerusalem. It will be built where the Dome of the Rock stands, or right beside it. The Dome of the Rock is a sacred Muslim shrine. It may be destroyed or it may be part of the division of Jerusalem that will be a part of the treaty, because the Bible says that the city of Jerusalem will be divided.

5. A ONE WORLD GOVERNMENT

The Bible says that there will be a one-world government, a one-world economy, a one-world leader who will come in as a peace-maker and then will persecute anyone who defies him.

6. THE ANTICHRIST

The Bible describes the Antichrist as arrogant and deceitful. Someone who will have a hypnotic affect on people. He will speak arrogantly and blasphemously. He will come in peacefully, as the negotiator of the peace treaty between Israel and the Palestinians but will soon be inhabited by Satan himself. He will tell people what they want to hear, but will break his promises, demanding complete obedience and worship. He will sit in the temple in Jerusalem proclaiming himself God.

7. THE FALSE PROPHET

The antichrist and the false prophet will be in control of the whole world, causing all to worship the antichrist and the devil. The false prophet will make an image of the beast and make it appear to come alive. He will pretend to accept all faiths and create a one-world religion.

8. THE MARK OF THE BEAST

All people will be commanded to take a mark on their right hand or forehead to be able to buy and sell. The chip is already available. It has been placed in animals and in some people.

9. TWO WITNESSES

God will soon send two prophets to warn of the coming judgment. They will be so hated by everyone that, when they are finally killed by the Antichrist, people around the world will celebrate. The prophets will lie on the street in Jerusalem for three and a half days before being raised up into the heavens.

10. BABYLON DESTROYED

Babylon will be destroyed. Which Babylon is the question. The real Babylon? Is this where the antichrist will set up his capitol? On the banks of the Tigris and Euphrates Rivers? Saddam Hussein tried to rebuild it but he didn't get very far.

Jerusalem was called a spiritual Babylon at one time. Rome, the center of the Roman Catholic Church, fits the description and sets on seven hills. Financial Babylon could be New York City, but an economic crisis may have already destroyed Wall Street and our ability to be a financial power.

11. INVASION FROM THE EAST

According to Revelation 9, China and the countries from the east will also try to take over the Middle East. Remember Turkey, which is very unstable, controls the dam on the Euphrates River and has just put down a major coup attempt, giving more power to a very strong Muslim president. Anyone could use that dam over the Euphrates River to dry up the river so that the two hundred million man army can march over to start World War III. One third of the world's people will be annihilated at that time

12. THE JEWS ESCAPE

The Jews who have been saved during the Tribulation period, will have to run for their lives because the devil, in the form of the Antichrist, will try to destroy them. The Bible says that they will be flown on the wings of an eagle. Could that possibly be the United States, (symbolized by an eagle,) assisting Israel? We pray that it is.

13. JESUS RETURNS WITH HIS ARMY TO FIGHT FOR ISRAEL

14. BE READY!

I know. I know. You do not want to hear it. You want to have your life, your marriage, your family, your home. But, how do I answer to God if I do not warn you of what is about to happen. I want to make sure that you have all asked Jesus to save you and have a relationship with Him that will keep you through anything.

"So Christ was once offered to bear the sins of many; and unto them that eagerly wait for him shall he appear the second time without sin unto salvation. " Hebrews 9:28

CHAPTER 2

WHAT DID JESUS SAY?
Is it the end of the world?

Matthew 24 gives us an overview of what is happening in the world at the end times. As he sat upon the Mount of Olives, the disciples came to him privately, saying, "Tell us,

1. When shall these things be?

2. And what shall be the sign of your coming,

3. And the end of the world?"

Matthew 24:4 "Jesus answered: 'Watch out that no one deceives you. For many will come in my name, claiming, 'I am the Messiah,' and will deceive many. 6 You will hear of wars and rumors of wars, but see to it that you are not alarmed. Such things must happen, but the end is still to come. 7 Nation will rise against nation, and kingdom against kingdom. There will be famines and earthquakes in various places. 8 All these are the beginning of birth pains.

Matthew 24:9 Then you will be handed over to be persecuted and put to death, and you will be hated by all nations because of me. 10 At that time many will turn away from the faith and will betray and hate each other. 11 and many false prophets will appear and deceive many people. 12 Because of the increase of wickedness, the love of most will grow cold. 13 but the one who stands firm to the end will be saved. 14 And this gospel of the kingdom will be preached in the whole world as a testimony to all nations, and then the end will come."

Matthew 24:32 "Now learn this lesson from the fig tree: As soon as its twigs get tender and its leaves come out, you know that summer is near. 33 Even so, when you see all these things, you know that it is near, right at the door. 34 Truly I tell you, this generation will certainly not pass away until all these things have happened"

Who is the fig tree? Many commentators believe that Israel is the fig tree and when Israel became a nation again, it began the "last generation." I think that is true but I find only two references where the people of Israel are compared to figs and which might give the impression that Israel is the fig tree: *Jeremiah 24:5 "This is what the Lord, the God of Israel, says: ' Like these good figs, I regard as good the exiles from Judah, whom I sent away from this place to the land of the Babylonians.'" Hosea 9:10 "When I found Israel, it was like finding grapes in the desert; when I saw your ancestors, it was like seeing the early fruit on the fig tree."*

This generation has seen the rebirth of Israel and all of the other conditions he told us would occur right before His second coming. So get ready. Jesus is coming!

Revelation 6 describes what are called the four horsemen of the Apocalypse and parallels much of Jesus' discourse in Matthew 24.

1.<u>Antichrists to deceive</u> - **white** *horse Rev. 6:2 And I saw, and behold a white horse and he that sat on him had a bow; and a crown was given unto him: and he went forth conquering, and to conquer.*

Matthew 24: 5 Many shall come in my name <u>saying, I am Christ; and shall deceive many</u>. There shall be many false Christs and false prophets. Indeed, false messiahs are everywhere, from Oprah to the Imams.

2. <u>Wars and rumors of wars</u> – **red** *horse Rev. 6:4 And there went out another horse that was red: and power was given to him that sat thereon to take peace* *from the earth, and that they should kill one another: and there was given unto him a great sword.*

Matthew 24: 6 And you shall hear of wars and rumors of wars: see that you are not troubled: for all these things must come to pass, but the end is not yet. 7a For nation shall rise against nation, and kingdom against kingdom..............

As of this writing, there were 67 countries involved in wars, 721 militias-guerrillas and terrorist-separatist-anarchic groups involved.

3. **Economic chaos and lack – black** *horse Revelation 6:5 And when he had opened the third seal, I heard the third beast say, Come and see. And I beheld, and lo a black horse; and he that sat on him had a pair of balances in his hand. And I heard a voice in the midst of the four beasts say, a measure of wheat for a penny, and three measures of barley for a penny; and see that you hurt not the oil and the wine.*

Inflation - A measure of wheat might feed a family for one meal. Three measures of barley, which were usually crops to feed livestock, would be cheaper and would feed a family perhaps for a day. But not hurting the oil and wine signify that some will be very rich while others will not have enough to buy food. That is one of the sins of America today, gluttony prevails in our land while so many in the world are starving to death.

4. **Death by famine, plague, sword, disease – pale** *horse Rev. 6:8 And I looked, and behold a pale horse: and his name that sat on him was Death, and Hades followed with him. And authority was given unto them over the fourth part of the earth, to kill with sword, and with hunger, and with death, and with the animals of the earth.*

Matthew 24: 7b and there shall be famines, and pestilences, and earthquakes in various places. 8 All these are the beginning of birth pains.

Famines

Including the 1959 Great Chinese Famine where there were 15 – 43 million deaths, the North Korean Famine in 1996, of 3.5 million, the Ethiopian famine of 1984-85, the Second Congo War famine that started in 1998, which killed 3.8 million, approximately 30 million people have died in the Twentieth Century. Many famines came because of weather disasters, but most of the famines came as a product or aftermath of war.

Plagues

Cholera has killed thousands world-wide. Smallpox was responsible for an estimated 300–500 million deaths in the 20th century. Malaria causes approximately one to three million deaths annually — this represents at least one death every 30 seconds, and Acquired Immune Deficiency Syndrome (AIDS) has led to the deaths of more than 25 million people since it was first recognized in 1981. That doesn't even include cancer's 8.2 million, at last count in 2012.

Earthquakes

Rev. 6:12 "And I beheld when he had opened the sixth seal, and lo, there was a great earthquake;..."

Matt. 24:7 "....and earthquakes in various places."

We have seen so many earthquakes, we are not even shocked anymore. Are they increasing in frequency?

The world's deadliest earthquakes since 2000

Jan. 26, 2001: A magnitude 7.7 quake strikes Gujarat in India, killing 20,000 people

Dec. 26, 2003: A magnitude 6.6 earthquake hits southeastern Iran, resulting in 50,000 deaths.

Dec. 26, 2004: A magnitude 9.1 quake in Indonesia triggers an Indian Ocean tsunami, killing 230,000 people in a dozen countries.

Oct. 8, 2005: A magnitude 7.6 earthquake kills over 80,000 people in Pakistan's Kashmir region.

May 12, 2008: A magnitude 7.9 quake strikes eastern Sichuan in China, resulting in over 87,500 deaths.

Jan. 12, 2010: A magnitude 7.0 quake hits Haiti, killing up to 316,000 people according to government estimates.

March 11, 2011: A magnitude 9.0 quake off the northeast coast of Japan triggers a tsunami, killing more than 20,000 people.

Source: U.S. Geological Survey

"Volcanic Activity and Earthquakes Have Increased Enormously Worldwide" Published on May 23, 2014 jamal shrair energy researcher at green energy visions

"Earthquakes and volcanic activity have increased worldwide. In 2013 10 major volcanoes along the ring of fire became active. The USGS has been strangely silent about this. http://www.activistpost.com/2013/11/why-have-10-major-volcanoes-along-ring.html. At the same time land and underwater volcanoes on the planet are awakening in record numbers. Unrest is growing among the world's supervolcanoes like Yellowstone and Long Valley calderas in the U.S, Laguna del Maule in Chile, Santorini in Greece, Campi Flegrei in Italy. Almost all of the world's active supervolcanoes are now exhibiting clear sign of inflation which is an indication that an eruption will take place in the near future."

"On the other hand, if we just look at earthquake activity in parts of the US like Oklahoma the picture would become clear. According to the Oklahoma Geological Survey, since 2009, the "earthquake activity in Oklahoma has been approximately 40 times higher than in the previous 30 years."

November 8, 2016 - "The USGS recorded 1,010 earthquakes of a magnitude 3.0 or greater in the region last year, nearly three times as many as the 318 temblors of this magnitude in 2009. Oklahoma alone felt 619 quakes of a magnitude 2.8 or larger from January through June of this year."

5. Persecution of Christians *Rev. 6:9 "And when he had opened the fifth seal, I saw under the altar the souls of them that were slain for the word of God, and for the testimony which they held:" Rev. 6: 11 "...rest yet for a little while, until their fellow servants also and their brethren, that should be killed as they were, should be fulfilled*

Matt. 24:9 "Then shall they deliver you up to be afflicted, and shall kill you: and you shall be hated of all nations for my name's sake." 100,000 Christians are killed annually. They are being abducted and executed in the most barbaric ways imaginable: buried alive, crucified, beheaded, burned, and worse. This has been going on in other countries for thousands of years but, finally, even America is beginning to notice the persecution of Christians around the world.

6. A Falling Away *2 Thessalonians 2:3 Let no man deceive you by any means: for that day* (the rapture) *shall not come, except there come a falling away first, and that man of sin be revealed, the son of perdition." Matthew 24: 10 "At that time many will turn away from the faith and will betray and hate each other."* Churches are closing by the hundreds and Christians feel no need to attend.

7. Increase of wickedness, lawlessness everywhere. ***Matt. 24:12 "And because lawlessness shall abound, the love of many shall grow cold."*** A woman in South Carolina has been arrested on murder charges after she allegedly put her newborn baby in the refrigerator for hours. "There were ten people at the home when the child died," an officer said. He was horrified of course but that is just one example of the atrocities that people, even mothers, are committing against their own children. There are so many more stories about mothers killing their babies, including almost 60 million that have been murdered by abortion.

Headline: **<u>Abortion Clinics Fighting to Keep Doing Dismemberment Abortions Tearing Off Baby's Limbs</u> Chilling Evidence Shows Planned Parenthood Selling Body Parts: "How's the Pancreas Forecast Today?"** A new batch of evidence from the Congressional panel investigating Planned Parenthood reveals that there are actually people involved in selling aborted baby body parts.

8. <u>The Gospel **Preached**</u> ***Matt. 24:14 "And this gospel of the kingdom shall be preached in all the world for a witness to all nations; and then shall the end come."*** This is one that could not have happened until the church was started two thousand years ago and even then, it would have been only in the area of the Roman world. Now, through satellite and television, it is being preached throughout the world.

Matthew24: 33 "So likewise, when you shall see all these things: (Israel's Return, many deceivers, wars and rumors of wars, famines, pestilences, earthquakes, persecution, love grown cold, the Gospel preached in all the world,) ***know that it is near, even at the doors. 34 Verily I say to you, This generation shall not pass, till all these things be fulfilled.***

CHAPTER 3

World Governments at the End of the Age

When King Nebuchadnezzar of Babylon had a dream, it was a prophetic dream that Daniel interpreted and it gave a description of world governments including Babylon, Media-Persia, Greece, Rome, and finally, a coalition of countries that would not hold together well. All of these but the last have been prominent on the world's stage and the last one, the mixture of iron and clay is possibly the European Union, which will not stay together. After that, God's kingdom will be set up forever.

God gave Daniel the interpretation, so we do not have to guess about what the dream meant.

Daniel 2:37 Your Majesty, you are the king of kings. The God of heaven has given you dominion and power and might and glory; 38 in your hands he has placed all mankind and the beasts of the field and the birds in the sky. Wherever they live, he has made you ruler over them all. You are that head of gold.

39 After you, another kingdom will arise, inferior to yours. Next, a third kingdom, one of bronze, will rule over the whole earth. 40 Finally, there will be a fourth kingdom, strong as iron—for iron breaks and smashes everything—and as iron breaks things to pieces, so it will crush and break all the others. 41 Just as you saw that the feet and toes were partly of baked clay and partly of iron, so this will be a divided kingdom; yet it will have some of the strength of iron in it, even as you saw iron missed with clay. 42 As the toes were partly iron and partly clay, so this kingdom will be partly strong and partly brittle. 43 And just as you saw the iron mixed with baked clay, so the people will be a mixture and ***will not remain united,*** *any more than iron mixes with clay.*

Daniel 2:44 "In the time of those kings, the God of heaven will set up a kingdom that will never be destroyed, nor will it be left to another people. It will crush all those kingdoms and bring them to an end, but it will itself endure forever. 45 This is the meaning of the vision of the rock cut out of a mountain, but not by human hands –a rock that broke the iron, the bronze, the clay, the silver and the gold to pieces. The great God has shown the king what will take place in the future. The dream is true and its interpretation is trustworthy."

The head of gold represents the Babylonian Empire, (Babylon ruled the world from 606 B.C to 538 B.C.) ; the silver chest and arms, the Media-Persian Empire established by Cyrus in 539 B.C., (Media-Persia ruled from 538 B.C. to 331 B.C.); the bronze belly and thighs, the Greek Empire established by Alexander the Great around 330 B.C., (Greece ruled from 331 B.C. to 168 B.C.); the iron legs and feet, the Roman Empire, (Rome ruled from 168 B.C. to 476 A.D.)

The toes represent a confederation of states occupying the territory formerly controlled by the Roman Empire. The feet and toes mixed of iron and clay, which are partly strong and partly brittle, represent the last earthly empire, perhaps a mixture of church and state, or just a combination of different countries, that will be broken in pieces by Christ, "the solid rock." His kingdom, is the everlasting kingdom that the saints will possess at the end of time when Jesus returns.

Since the larger prophecy has come true in every respect, it only makes sense to expect the last part of it to come true. The European Union, from which Britain exited last year, may be the feet of iron and clay which cannot remain united, but may morph into the One World Government composed of ten areas. I believe it will be the Roman Catholic Church which will combine with other religions and share, for a time, authority with the world leader and the political rulers of those ten areas. The exciting part of the prophecy is that the "Rock," Jesus, will crush all of the feet and toes and Christ's kingdom will begin.

CHAPTER 4

World Systems at the End of the Age

We know that the horses and riders of Revelation 6 are symbols of end-times conditions, but could they also **represent world systems that are in place in the end times era?** What if these are demon spirits loosed upon the earth in the form of systems that are currently in place?

1. White horse *Rev. 6:2 And I saw, and behold a white horse and he that sat on him had a bow; and a crown was given unto him: and he went forth conquering, and to conquer.* **Antichrists to deceive - white horse.** Could the white horse represent Catholicism? For instance, the Catholic pope usually wears white and often a crown. This man on the white horse means to conquer with a bow without arrows. What does that mean? Could it mean that he will conquer without having to use weapons? The deception is that the pope is considered in place of God on earth. The Catholic Church has been a world system throughout the last two centuries.

2. Red horse *Rev. 6:4 And there went out another horse that was red: and power was given to him that sat thereon to take peace from the earth, and that they should kill one another: and there was given unto him a great sword.* **Wars and rumors of wars – red horse.** Could the red horse represent Communism? They have killed millions of people over the last century and are still killing to retain dominance in countries around the world.

3. **Black horse** *Rev. 6:5 And when he had opened the third seal, I heard the third beast say, Come and see. And I beheld, and lo a black horse; and he that sat on him had a pair of balances in his hand. And I heard a voice in the midst of the four beasts say, a measure of wheat for a penny, and three measures of barley for a penny; and see that you hurt not the oil and the wine.* **Economic chaos and lack – black horse.** Could the black horse represent capitalism and inflation, with its disparity between wealth and poverty?

4. Pale (choler) horse *Rev. 6:8 And I looked, and behold a pale horse: and his name that sat on him was Death, and Hades followed with him. And authority was given unto them over the fourth part of the earth, to kill with sword, and with hunger, and with death, and with the animals of the earth.* **Death by famine, plague, sword, animals. In Greek, the word used for this horse, "pale," is chloros. (5515, Strong's) This word properly means "pale-green, like the color of the first shoots of grass, then green, verdant.** Could the pale green (chloros) horse represent Islam? Twenty-seven per cent of the world's population are Muslim. On banners, on doors, on gates, and railings, wherever they are established, their color is green. Muslims are known for using swords to behead their enemies, but wherever they make war, famine follows.

CHAPTER 5

Nations at the End of the Age

As we come to the end of the age, we discover more light to the prophecies. It now appears to some commentators that the beast in Daniel 7 may represent not four historic kingdoms, but instead nations that are in place in the last generations. It makes sense that there would not need to be a duplication depicting the world empires when they have already been named. So, consider the possibility of these beasts representing four nations present at the end of the ages.

Daniel 7:3 "And four great beasts came up from the sea, different one from another. 4 The first was like a lion, and had eagle's wings: I beheld till the wings were plucked off, and it was lifted up from the earth, and made stand upon the feet as a man, and a man's heart was given to it." Doesn't that sound like Great Britain, whose national symbol is the lion, and the United States, whose national symbol is the eagle and evolved to be represented by Uncle Sam?

5 "And behold another beast, a second, like to a bear, and it was raised up on one side, and it had three ribs in the mouth of it between the teeth of it: and they said to it, Arise, devour much flesh."

Russia, whose national symbol is the bear, has murdered millions, and is rising again.

6 "After this I beheld, and lo another, like a leopard, which had upon the back of it four wings of a fowl; the beast had also four heads; and dominion was given to it."

I wondered which country was represented by a leopard, thinking it was probably an Islamic country, but it could be Germany. Some commentators suggest that the four heads of the leopard represent the first, second and third Reichs of Germany and that the fourth is to come soon. Germany has a close alliance to France, which has a rooster, (a fowl,) as its symbol.

7 "After this I saw in the night visions, and behold a fourth beast, dreadful and terrible, and strong exceedingly; and it had great iron teeth: it devoured and brake in pieces and trampled the residue with the feet of it: and it was different from all the beasts that were before it; and it had ten horns."

This would be the government that takes over the world. Just as the statue that started with a gold head representing Babylon in Daniel 2 and went through the world kingdoms until it got to the feet that were iron and clay mixed and had ten toes, this last government consists of ten divisions of the world.

Iron represented Rome, so it could mean the revival of the Holy Roman Empire. The European Union was formed by the "Club of Rome" when they signed the "Treaty of Rome." As the old Holy Roman Empire was a mix of European monarchs and the Roman Catholic papacy, this conglomeration of countries may have as the iron mouthpiece, the Roman Catholic pope, who speaks for the Antichrist, the "little horn."

Daniel 7:8 *"While I was thinking about the horns,* (the kings and kingdoms) *there before me was another horn, a little one,* (the Antichrist) *which came up among them; and three of the first horns* (three kingdoms which will fall to the Antichrist) *were uprooted before it. This horn had eyes like the eyes of a human being and a mouth that spoke boastfully." (Not to fear, we discover quickly what will happen to the Antichrist.)*

Daniel 7:11-12 *"Then I continued to watch because of the boastful words the horn (the Antichrist) was speaking. I kept looking until the beast was slain and its body destroyed and thrown into the blazing fire. The other beasts had been stripped of their authority, but were allowed to live for a period of time." (*Does this mean that the other powers will exist for a while after the Antichrist is killed and sent to Hell?)

Daniel 7:13-14 *"I saw in the night visions, and, behold, one like the Son of man (Jesus) came with the clouds of heaven, and came to the Ancient of days, (God) and they brought him near before him.* **14** *And there was given him dominion, and glory, and a kingdom, that all people, nations, and languages, should serve him: his dominion is an everlasting dominion, which shall not pass away, and his kingdom that which shall not be destroyed."* Again, this makes me think that this chapter has to refer to the last days and countries that exist now.

Daniel 7:19-22 *"Then I wanted to know the meaning of the fourth beast, (the conglomeration of world powers) which was different from all the others and most terrifying…."*

One of the angels interpreted the dream for Daniel. This definitely refers to the last days.

Daniel 7:23-26 "He gave me this explanation: The fourth beast is a fourth kingdom that will appear on earth. It will be different from all the other kingdoms and will devour the whole earth, *(a one world government,) trampling it down and crushing it. The ten horns are ten kings (ten divisions of the world government,) who will come from this kingdom. After them another king (the Antichrist) will arise, different from the earlier ones; he will subdue three kings. (three divisions and their rulers) He will speak against the Most High* (God) *and oppress his holy people* (Israel or those saved during the tribulation period?*) and try to change the set times and the laws. The holy people will be delivered into his hands for a time, times and half a time* (three and a half years.)

But the court will sit, and his power will be taken away and completely destroyed forever. Then the sovereignty, power and greatness of all the kingdoms under heaven will be handed over to the holy people of the Most High. His kingdom will be an everlasting kingdom, and all rulers will worship and obey him

Daniel 7:27 *"And the kingdom and dominion, and the greatness of the kingdom under the whole heaven, shall be given to the people of the saints of the most High, whose kingdom is an everlasting kingdom, and all dominions shall serve and obey him."*

Revelation 17:12 *The ten horns you saw are ten kings* (global leaders over ten divisions of the world,) *who have not yet received a kingdom, but who for one hour will receive authority as kings along with the beast....14 They will wage war against the Lamb, (Jesus,) but the Lamb will triumph over them because he is the Lord of Lords and King of king --- and with him will be his called, chosen and faithful followers.*

We see the end of the story. The Lamb is triumphant and we who are Christians, the called, chosen and faithful saints of the most High, will receive an everlasting kingdom with God.

CHAPTER 6

Moral Climate at the End of the Age

2 Timothy 3:1 This know also, that in the last days perilous (DANGEROUS) *times shall come.*

2 Peter 3:3 Knowing this first, that there shall come in the last days scoffers, walking after their own lusts, 4 and saying, Where is the promise of his coming? For since the fathers fell asleep, all things continue as they were from the beginning of the creation.

Jude 18 How that they told you there should be mockers in the last time, who should walk after their own ungodly lusts. 19 These are they who cause divisions, worldly, having not the Spirit.

2 Peter 3:8 But, beloved, be not ignorant of this one thing, that one day is with the Lord as a thousand years, and a thousand years as one day. 9 The Lord is not slack concerning his promise, as some men count slackness: but is long-suffering toward us, not willing that any should perish, but that all should come to repentance.

2 Peter 3:10 But the day of the Lord will come as a thief in the night; in the which the heavens shall pass away with a great noise, and the elements shall melt with fervent heat, the earth also and the works that are therein shall be burned up.

Daniel 12:4 ..."Seal the book, even to the time of the end: many shall run to and fro, and knowledge shall be increased."

Are there other world events occurring today that have significance with what the Bible prophesies? How many? Are they major signs? Do they pertain to the Biblical descriptions of "last day" conditions?

CURRENT EVENTS

- ✓ Israel is surrounded by enemies.
- ✓ Russia is rising.
- ✓ Russia's allies are Iran, Libya, Turkey, Ethiopia, etc.
- ✓ Russia is moving toward the Middle East.
- ✓ North Korea, China are negotiating with Russia.
- ✓ China is building a road to the Middle East.
- ✓ The United States is weakening.
- ✓ A cashless society is on the horizon.
- ✓ The countries surrounding Israel are bombing them continually and threatening annihilation.
- ✓ A peace treaty for Israel is constantly being negotiated.
- ✓ Terrorists are at work in every country.
- ✓ Muslims are beheading anyone who does not accept their beliefs.
- ✓ Computers can contain information about every person on earth.
- ✓ Identification chips can be implanted in objects, animals and people for tracking purposes.
- ✓ Global positioning systems can locate any vehicle or cell phone.
- ✓ Technology can put televised events all over the world as they occur.
- ✓ There is an increase of tornadoes.

- ✓ There is an increase of earthquakes.
- ✓ There is an increase of hurricanes and storms.
- ✓ Plagues are increasing: cancer, Ebola, Aids.
- ✓ Increasing famine
- ✓ The Falling away of the church
- ✓ Increasing immorality
- ✓ Increasing persecution of Christians
- ✓ Mothers killing their babies
- ✓ Gospel being preached by satellite

CHAPTER 7

Jesus, Prophecy Fulfilled

If you need to be convinced that the prophecies of the Bible are true, you need only look at the prophecies of Jesus' life that were fulfilled.

1. Jesus to be born of a Virgin

Isaiah 7:14 "Therefore the Lord himself shall give you a sign; Behold a virgin shall conceive, and bear a son, and shall call his name Immanuel, (God with us)."

Matthew 1:18 "This is how the birth of Jesus Christ came about: His mother Mary......was found to be with child through the Holy Spirit."

2. Jesus to be born in Bethlehem

Micah 5:2 "But you, Bethlehem Ephrata, though you are little among the thousands of Judah, yet out of you shall he come forth unto me that is to be ruler in Israel; whose goings forth have been from of old, from everlasting."

Matthew 2:1 "After Jesus was born in Bethlehem in Judea, during the time of King Herod, Magi from the east came to Jerusalem...."

3. He would be preceded by a Messenger.

Isaiah 40:3 "A voice of one calling: 'In the desert prepare thc way for the Lord; make straight in the wilderness a highway for our God.'"

Matthew 3:1-2 "In those days John the Baptist came, preaching in the Desert of Judea and saying, 'Repent, for the kingdom of heaven is near.'"

4, Jesus was rejected.

Isaiah 53: 3-7 "He is despised and rejected of men: a man of sorrows, and acquainted with grief: and we hid as it were our faces from him; he was despised, and we esteemed him not. Surely he has borne our griefs, and carried our sorrows: yet we did esteem him stricken, smitten of God, and afflicted.

John 7:5 "For even his own brothers did not believe in him." John 1:11 He came unto his own, but his own did not receive him."

5. He was the Passover Lamb.

Isaiah 53:7 He was oppressed, and he was afflicted, yet he opened not his mouth; he is brought as a lamb to the slaughter, and as a sheep before her hearers is dumb, so he opened not his mouth.

1 Corinthians 5:7 Get rid of the old leaven......for Christ, our Passover lamb, has been sacrificed."

6. He was crucified.

In Psalm 22:12-18, we have a detailed description of the crucifixion. It was written 1000 years before Jesus was born. At that time, crucifixion hadn't even been invented.

Even the fact of the soldiers gambling over his clothes was included in the prophecy.

Psalm 22:16 "Dogs surround me, a pack of villains encircles me; they pierce my hands and my feet. All my bones are on display; people stare and gloat over me. They divide my clothes among them and cast lots for my garment."

John 19:23 "When the soldiers crucified Jesus, they took his clothes, dividing them into four shares, one for each of them with the undergarment remaining. This garment was seamless, woven in one piece from tope to bottom. 24 'Let's not tear it,' they said to one another. 'Let's decide by lot who will get it.'"

7. His side was pierced.

Zechariah 12:10 "They will look on me, the one they have pierced, and they will mourn for him as one mourns for an only child, and grieve bitterly for him as one mourns for an only son.

John 19:34 "Instead, one of the soldiers pierced Jesus' side with a spear, bringing a sudden flood of blood and water.

8. His burial site was prophesied.

Isaiah 53:9 "And he made his grave with the wicked, and with the rich in his death; because he had done no violence, neither was any deceit in his mouth

Matthew 27:57 "As evening approached, there came a rich man from Arimathea, named Joseph, ...he asked for Jesus' body..and placed it in his own new tomb."

Peter Stoner in Science Speaks (Moody Press, 1963,) says that by using the modern science of probability in reference to just eight of the prophecies, "we find that the chance that any man might have lived down to the present time and fulfilled all eight prophecies is 1 in 10^{17}." That would be 1 in 100,000,000,000,000,000.

Stoner considers 48 prophecies about Jesus and says, "we find the chance that any one man fulfilled all 48 prophecies to be 1 in 10^{157}, or 1 in

100,000,000,000,000,000,000,000,000,000,000,000,000,000,000,000,
000,000,000,000,000,000,000,000,000,000,000,000,000,000,000,000,000,00
0,000,000,000,000, 000, 000,000,000,000,000,000,000,000,000,000,000,000
,000.

When you consider the accuracy of the prophecies about Jesus, it is hard to dispute that the future prophecies will also be fulfilled. But if you are still skeptical, then consider the history of Israel.

CHAPTER 8

Israel, the Key to Prophecy

Queen Victoria once asked her Jewish prime minister the following question, "Can you give me just one verse in the Bible to prove that it's true?" He replied, "Your majesty, I can give you one word -- the Jew!"

If you have a hard time believing the Bible about future prophecies, just study the prophecies that have already come to pass. The following are only a few of the Old Testament Prophecies about the nation of Israel that have been fulfilled.

1. The temple was destroyed by the Romans.

Matthew 24:1,2 "And Jesus went out, and departed from the temple: and his disciples came to him to show him the buildings of the temple. And Jesus said to them, 'Do you see all these things? Verily I say to you, There shall not be left here one stone upon another, that shall not be thrown down.'" This happened when the Romans destroyed it and, to get the gold between the stones, they broke every one of them apart.

2. The Jews were scattered all over the world.

Deuteronomy 28: 64-66 The Lord will scatter you among all peoples, from one end of the earth to the other....And among these nations you shall find no ease, and there shall be no rest for the sole of your foot...night and day you shall be in dread, and have no assurance of your life...

Thirty years after Jesus was crucified, the Jews rebelled against Rome. The Roman army besieged and captured Jerusalem, filling the streets with corpses and destroying the temple. After sixty years, there was another revolt and the Romans, determined to stop the revolts, sold the Jews into slavery and they were taken to all parts of the world.

3. Israel became a nation again on May 14, 1948.

Isaiah 66:8,9 "Who has heard such a thing? Who has seen such things? Shall the earth be made to give birth in one day? Or shall a nation be born at once? For as soon as Zion travailed, she brought forth her children."

When my mother was born, in 1920, no one dreamed that Israel would ever become a nation again. The preachers explained the Bible verses that prophesied about it by saying that the church was substituted for Israel in those passages. But, on May 14, 1948, Israel was re-born and was given nation status.

Headline: **After 1,878 Years Israel Becomes A Nation Again May 14, 1948**

4. Israel is re-gathered.

Ezekiel 37:21-22 …I will take the Israelites out of the nations where they have gone. I will gather them from all around and bring them back into their own land. I will make them one nation in the land, on the mountains of Israel. There will be one king over all of them and they will never again be two nations or be divided into two kingdoms.

Ezekiel 37:11-12 Then he said to me: "Son of man, these bones are the people of Israel. They say, 'Our bones are dried up and our hope is gone; we are cut off.

Therefore prophesy and say to them: "This is what the Sovereign Lord says: My people, I am going to open your graves and bring you up from them; I will bring you back to the Land of Israel."

Isaiah 11:12 And he shall set up an ensign for the nations, and shall assemble the outcasts of Israel, and gather together the dispersed of Judah from the four corners of the earth.

Ezekiel 11:17 Therefore say, Thus says the Lord God; I will even gather you from the people, and assemble you out of the countries where you have been scattered, and I will give you the land of Israel.

Hosea 1:10 Yet the number of the children of Israel shall be as the sand of the sea, which cannot be measured nor numbered; and it shall come to pass, that in the place where it was said to them, You are not my people, there it shall be said to them, You are the sons of the living God.

Three times the number of Jews sent out of Israel and dispersed to the far corners of earth have returned to Israel. 1.3 million Jews have come from Russia at this time and thousands from around the world.

Headline, May 24, 1994 – **15 Thousand Ethiopian Jews Airlifted To Israel On 42 Aircraft In 24 Hours!**

5. Hebrew is Israel's national language.

During a tour, a guard in a museum in Israel, bent over and read a Hebrew text for the tourists, commenting that no other ancient language could be read by a common person, but Israelis can still read their ancient texts.

Zephaniah 3:9 For then will I restore to the people a pure language, that they may all call upon the name of the Lord, to serve him with one accord.

No matter which nation they came out of, they all learned Hebrew, their ancient language. Eliezer Ben Yehuda was vilified in life for collecting material for the dictionary of an ancient language, which today is the national language of Israel.

5. Israel has reclaimed the land.

Amos 9:14,15 "And I will bring again the captivity of my people of Israel, and they shall build the waste cities, and inhabit them; and they shall plant vineyards, and drink the wine thereof; they shall also make gardens, and eat the fruit of them. And I will plant them upon their land, and they shall no more be pulled up out of their land which I have given them, says the Lord your God."

Resettlement for the Jews in their land has not been easy. They have fought many wars, most of which were miracles of God's intervention, to regain the land. These are the main ones:

War of Independence (1948–1949) Arab invasion of Israel repelled.

1949 Armistice Agreements; Israel kept the area allotted to it by the Partition Plan and captured 50% of area allotted to Arab state

Sinai War (1956) Sinai demilitarized, UNEF deployed.

Six-Day War (1967) Israel captured the Gaza Strip, Sinai, the West Bank, and the Golan Heights

War of Attrition (1969–1970) Continued Israeli occupation of Sinai

Yom Kippur War (1973) Arab invasion of Israel repelled; UN ceasefire. Political gains for Egypt and Israel-Egypt–Israel Peace Treaty Israel–Syria Disengagement Agreement

Psalm 102 When the Lord shall build up Zion, he shall appear in his glory. **Zion, (Israel,) has been building up since 1948, so we can start looking for the Lord's appearance.**

6. The desert begins to bloom.

Isaiah 35:1 The wilderness and the desert place shall be glad for them; and the desert shall rejoice, and blossom as the rose.

Headline: Israelis Use Technology to Make the Desert Bloom

7. Israel reclaims the desolate land.

Isaiah 61:4 "And they shall build the old wastes, they shall raise up the former desolations, and they shall repair the ruined cities, the desolations of many strangers.

8. Israel has one government.

Ezekiel 37:21,22 "Thus says the Lord God; Behold, I will take the children of Israel from among the nations where they have gone, and will gather them on every side, and bring them into their own land: and I will make them one nation in the land upon the mountains of Israel; and one king shall be king to them all: and they shall be no more two nations, neither shall they be divided into two kingdoms any more at all."

Hosea 1:11 Then shall the children of Judah and the children of Israel be gathered together, and appoint themselves one head, and they shall come up out of the land: for great shall be the day of Jezreel.

9. Many nations have hated Jews and have tried to destroy them.

Deuteronomy 28:37 You shall become an astonishment, a proverb, and a byword among all nations where the Lord will drive you.

Headlines: "**Jews persecuted everywhere"**

"Europe's Anti-Semitism Comes Out of the Shadows" By Jim Yardley Sept. 23, 2014

"Anti-Semitism on rise across Europe 'in worst times since the Nazis'"

Headline: "Benjamin Netanyahu tells Europe's Jews to move to Israel, 'your home'

On his website Thursday, October 22, **Iranian President Mahmoud Ahmadinejad said, " the ultimate goal of world forces must be the annihilation of Israel."**

10. Jerusalem is at the middle of a world-wide controversy.

Zechariah 12:3 "And in that day I will make Jerusalem a heavy stone for all peoples: all that would heave it away shall be cut in pieces, though all the people of the earth be gathered together against it.

Surrounded by Arab states, the Israelis are being bombarded by the enemies around them and being betrayed by enemies abroad. So, to make peace, they have given away much of the land that they won back in the war with the Arabs. Still, not satisfied, the United Nations is pushing for more territory to be given to the Palestinians and for Jerusalem to be divided.

Ps. 83:2-4 "Your enemies make an uproar: and they that hate you have exalted themselves. They have taken crafty counsel against your people, and consulted against your sheltered ones. They have said, Come and let us cut them off from being a nation; that the name of Israel may be no more in remembrance." 5 For they have consulted together with one consent: they are confederate against thee:

Why is little Israel so important?

Jerusalem, "City of Peace," has been besieged about forty different times and destroyed (at least partially) on thirty-two different occasions. She has been fought over by armies of the Assyrians, Babylonians, Egyptians, Greeks, Ptolemies, Seleucids, Romans, Byzantines, Persians, Arabs, Seljuks, Crusaders, Mongols, Mamelukes, by the Turks, the British, and the Jordanians.

Jerusalem is sacred to three religions: Judaism, Christianity, and Islam. It is an open secret that the Pope desires to set up his world headquarters there, having claimed for many years that the Holy Land has all along really been under Roman Catholic "stewardship." So, with the whole world watching a piece of land that is a little larger than New Jersey, you wonder why Israel cannot keep just this little part of the land that God promised them. How have they survived this long? What will their enemies do next? Can there be peace?

CHAPTER 9

The Peace Treaty/ Russian Invasion

There is going to be a big blow-up in the Middle East. It has to be something really tremendous because it will necessitate a peace treaty between the Jews and the Palestinians. World leaders have been trying to hammer that out for years to no avail, so something has to happen that will make all parties consent. The Arabs surround Israel and they would much rather just blow Israel off the map, so what would make them agree?

Headline: November 25, 2015 "***Kerry fears Israeli-Palestinian conflict may 'spin out of control'***"

Headline: June 3, 2016 ***"Israeli-Palestinian Peace Process***

"PARIS – Foreign ministers from 29 countries convened in Paris to demonstrate 'with policies and actions, a genuine commitment to the two-state solution in order to rebuild trust.'"

"The thirty nations were there for the purpose of producing a UN resolution that will find a final solution to the Middle East conflict. The main players are the United States, the European Union, Russia, and the United Nations. The foreign ministers agreed to hold an international conference to further push for a peace deal by the end of 2016, but did not set a date."

"Isaac Herzog is the leader of Israel's opposition, the Zionist Union and hopes to replace Benjamin Netanyahu as the prime minister of Israel. Before the elections of 2015, he signed a secret agreement with the Palestinians to create a Palestinian state in Judea-Samaria and to make Jerusalem a shared capital. It would also place the Temple Mount under international control. A highway and eco bridges have already been built that will be checkpoints for people to go between the divisions of Jerusalem."

Why is a peace treaty between Israel and the Palestinians so important? And who will be able to negotiate it?

Daniel 9:27: "And he, (the Antichrist,) *shall confirm the covenant,* (the peace treaty,) *with many for one week, (*a week of years*), and in the midst of the week* (after three and a half years,*) he shall cause the sacrifice and the oblation to cease."*

But it will be a false peace. The Lord spoke to His prophets several times when speaking of this time.

Jeremiah 6:14 They have healed also the hurt of the daughter of my people slightly, saying, Peace, peace; when there is no peace.

1 Thessalonians 5:3 For when they shall say, Peace and safety; then sudden destruction will come upon them, as travail upon a woman with child; and they shall not escape.

According to *Revelation 11:2*, the peace treaty will divide Jerusalem, *And there was given me a measuring rod like a staff: and the angel stood, saying Rise, and measure the temple of God, and the altar, and them that worship therein. 3. But the court which is outside the temple leave out, and do not measure it; for it is given to the Gentiles: and the holy city shall they tread under foot forty and two months.*

Zechariah 1:16 Therefore thus says the Lord; I am returned to Jerusalem with mercies: my house shall be built in it, says the Lord of hosts, and a surveyor's line shall be stretched forth upon Jerusalem.

So why would the Israelis agree to that? Why would the Palestinians agree to that? A temple is going to be built on the Temple Mount (the most dangerous square mile on the planet,) which is where the Muslim Dome of the Rock stands, so what will happen to that? The destruction of a major Islamic holy site would definitely trigger a major conflict in the Middle East

Jerusalem has been divided before. From May of 1948 until 1967, the city was divided by walls, barbed-wire fences and a strip of no-man's land that cut right through the heart of Jerusalem, excluding the Jews from the old city and the Temple Mount until it was recaptured in 1967.

On the third day of the Six Day War, the Temple Mount was re-taken. On June 7 of that year, the Israeli troops moved into the Old City and stood at the Western Wall (Wailing Wall) for prayer. The city of Jerusalem was reunified. But it is to be divided again for three and a half years during the tribulation.

The prophesied agreement will turn Judea into a Palestinian state. The United Nations voted on November 29, 2012, to recognize a Palestinian state within pre-1967 borders. This is the biblical area of Judea. As a result, Israel is now considered an occupying power in the eyes of the world community. If Israel doesn't come to terms with the Palestinians through negotiations, the Palestinians have already said they will file charges against Israel at the UN. Israel desperately wants to avoid a showdown with the entire world community.

Isaiah 28:14 "Therefore hear the word of the Lord, you scoffers who rule this people in Jerusalem, 15 You boast, 'We have entered into a covenant with death, with the grave we have made an agreement. When an overwhelming scourge sweeps by, it cannot touch us, for we have made a lie our refuge and falsehood our hiding place.'"

When the agreement is signed, the Temple Mount will be placed under a sharing arrangement between Muslims and Jews. Most people do not know that a law was introduced in the Israeli Knesset on November 1,

2013, to place the Temple Mount under a sharing arrangement so that both Jews and Muslims can worship there.

During the first three and one-half years after the agreement is signed, the Jews will build their temple on the Temple Mount.

In 2013 Israel's number one trading partner, the European Union, placed the settlements in Judea-Samaria under economic sanctions. No EU member is supposed to conduct trade with the West Bank settlers or with any Israeli entity that has any ties to the West Bank settlers. Many other countries and organizations are beginning to follow suit. Palestinian Leader Mahmoud Abbas has said that he will press charges against Israel and her leaders before the International Criminal Court if a peace agreement is not reached by April 29, 2014. This, of course, did not happen. But it will.

When a Palestinian-Israeli peace agreement is reached, the final seven years, the "tribulation," will begin. But the Great Tribulation, the last three and a half years, will begin when the Antichrist breaks the agreement and stands in the temple proclaiming himself to be God, and literally, all Hell will break loose.

Isaiah 28:18 And your covenant with death shall be annulled, and your agreement with hell shall not stand; when the overflowing scourge shall pass through, then you shall be trodden down by it.

Daniel 8:13-14 "Then I heard one saint speaking, and another saint said unto that certain saint which spoke, How long shall be the vision concerning the daily sacrifice, and the transgression of desolation, to give both the sanctuary and the host to be trodden under foot? 14 And he said unto me, Unto two thousand and three hundred days; then shall the sanctuary be cleansed."

When the treaty has been signed, and everyone is saying, "Peace and safety," I believe the Russians are going to start their "March to the South," which we discussed at the beginning of this book.

CHAPTER 10

"COME UP HERE!"

The Rapture

Luke 21:28 says "And when these things begin to come to pass, then look up, and lift up your heads; for your redemption draws near."

Acts 1:10-11 They were looking intently up into the sky as he was going, when suddenly two men dressed in white stood beside them. "Men of Galilee," they said, "why do you stand here looking into the sky? This same Jesus, who has been taken from you into heaven, will come back in the same way you have seen him go into heaven."

It is impossible for anyone to know when the church will be taken up in the air to be with the Lord. Some think it will be before the Tribulation starts. Some believe it will be in the middle. Some assert that it will be right before His coming back to earth. Different scriptures can be interpreted to prove each of those viewpoints. No one knows when, so it is imperative that we all be ready to go whenever it happens and be witnessing to the lost and be ready for persecution in the meantime.

The members of the church in Thessolonica were concerned because they had heard that the Return of Christ had already happened. So, Paul wrote a letter to assure them that the coming of the Lord could not occur until there was a falling away and the son of perdition was revealed. That son of perdition, the Antichrist, is going to sit in the temple and declare himself to be God.

1Thessalonians 2: 1-4 "Concerning the coming of our Lord Jesus Christ and our being gathered to him, we ask you, brothers and sisters, not to become easily unsettled or alarmed by the teaching allegedly from us – whether by a prophecy or by word of mouth or by letter – asserting that the day of the Lord has already come. Don't let anyone deceive you in any way, for that day will not come until the rebellion occurs and the man of lawlessness is revealed, the man doomed to destruction.

What kind of rebellion? It is likely that the Antichrist will be revealed when the peace treaty is signed.

He will oppose and will exalt himself over everything that is called God or is worshiped, so that he sets himself up in God's temple, proclaiming himself to be God."

We know the Antichrist will sit in the temple and declare himself to be God in the middle of the Tribulation, so this verse is one of the reasons that many think the rapture will not occur until this mid-point, but he would have already been recognized as the Antichrist before that by anyone who knew the Word of God.

Besides, that would mean that we would all be aware of the day that Christ would come for His Church, three and a half years into the Tribulation period, but *1Thessalonians 5: 2 says, " The day of the Lord comes as a thief in the night. This letter also says: 6. "Let us watch."*

The church will not know the day or the hour when the Lord will come to get us, but Jesus warned us to be watching and ready. Thankfully, verse *9 says, " God has not appointed us to wrath,"* (Revelation 6:17 calls the period of the Tribulation the day of his wrath.)

Matthew 24:36 "But of that day and hour knows no man, no, not the angels of heaven, but my Father only. 37 But as the days of Noah were, so shall also the coming of the Son of man be. 38 For as in the days that were before the flood they were eating and drinking, marrying and giving in marriage, until the day that Noah entered into the ark. 39 And knew not until the flood came, and took them all away; so shall also the coming of the Son of man be.

The rapture of the believers will be sudden and quick and for those who have lost loved ones, the promise that those who are dead in Christ shall rise first, should make us all rejoice.

1Thessalonians 4:16 The Lord himself shall descend from heaven with a shout, with the voice of the archangel and with the trump of God: and the dead in Christ shall rise first: 17 Then we which are alive and remain shall be caught up together with them in the clouds, to meet the Lord in the air: and so shall we ever be with the Lord. 18 Wherefore comfort one another with these words.

1 Corinthians 15:51-52 We shall all be changed, in a moment, in the twinkling of an eye, at the last trump: **(This, perhaps is the reason for some to believe that the church will not be raptured until the end.**) *for the trumpet shall sound, and the dead shall be raised incorruptible, and we shall be changed.*

It isn't likely that Jesus coming to get the saints would be the same as the "day of the Lord," when He will come with His saints to destroy His enemies and set up the judgment seat.

Matthew 24:40 Therefore keep watch, because you do not know on what day your Lord will come. 43 But understand this: If the owner of the house had known at what time of night the thief was coming, he would have kept watch and would not have let his house be broken into. 4 So you also must be ready, because the Son of Man will come at an hour when you do not expect him.

Luke 17:34 "I tell you, in that night there shall be two men in one bed; the one shall be taken, and the other shall be left. 35 Two women shall be grinding together; the one shall be taken, and the other left. 36 Two men shall be in the field; the one shall be taken, and the other left. 37 And they answered and said unto him, Where, Lord? And he said unto them, Wherever the body is, there will the eagles be gathered together.

The body of Christ will be caught up into the heavens, where the eagles are. We just do not know when. No one knows the day or hour. Think about it. The day and hour are different all over the globe. But you can know the season. It will be just like in Noah's days. Men will be eating and drinking, marrying and giving in marriage, oblivious to the signs of Christ's return while violence and evil will have taken over.

2 Peter 3: 5 But they deliberately forget that long ago by God's word the heavens came into being and the earth was formed out of water and by water. 6 By these waters also the world of that time was deluged and destroyed. 7 By the same word the present heavens and earth are reserved for fire, being kept for the day of judgment and destruction of the ungodly.

10 But the day of the Lord will come like a thief. The heavens will disappear with a roar; the elements will be destroyed by fire, and the earth and everything done in it will be laid bare. 13 But in keeping with his promise we are looking forward to a new heaven and a new earth, where righteousness dwells.

Daniel 12:4 ..."Seal the book, even to the time of the end: many shall run to and fro, and knowledge shall be increased."

Matthew 24:44 So you also must be ready because the Son of Man will come at an hour when you do not expect him.

CHAPTER 11

Israel's Spiritual Rebirth

Ezekiel says that the Russian confederation will be destroyed by God on the mountains of Israel. It will be a slaughter amidst a storm of monumental proportions, including hail, fire and brimstone.

Ezekiel 38:18 This is what will happen in that day: When Gog attacks the land of Israel, my hot anger will be aroused, declares the Sovereign Lord. 19 In my zeal and fiery wrath I declare that at that time there shall be a great earthquake in the land of Israel. 21 I will summon a sword against Gog on all my mountains, declares the Sovereign Lord. Every man's sword will be against his brother. 22 I will execute judgments on him with plague and bloodshed, I will pour down torrents of rain, hailstones and burning sulfur on him and on his troops and on the many nations with him. 23.....then they will know that I am the Lord.

Ezekiel 39:4 On the mountains of Israel you will fall, you and all your troops and the nations with you. 22 ..so the house of Israel shall know that I am the Lord their God from that day and forward.

Because of this miracle of intervention, the eyes of the Jews will be opened and they will realize that Jesus is the Messiah. As a nation, they will turn to God and the people of Israel will weep because they will finally realize that Jesus is their Messiah.

Ezekiel 36:25 I will sprinkle clean water on you, and you will be clean; I will cleanse you from all your impurities and from all your idols. 26 I will give you a new heart and put a new spirit in you; I will remove from you your heart of stone and give you a heart of flesh. 27 And I will put my Spirit in you and move you to follow my decrees and be careful to keep my laws.

Ezekiel 39:22 From that day forward the people of Israel will know that I am the Lord their God. 29 I will no longer hide my face from them, for I will pour out my Spirit on the people of Israel, declares the Sovereign Lord.

Zechariah 12:10 And I will pour upon the house of David, and upon the inhabitants of Jerusalem, the spirit of grace and of supplications: and they shall look upon me whom they have pierced, and they shall mourn for him, as one mourns for his only son, and shall be in bitterness for him, as one that is in bitterness for his first-born.

Zechariah13: 2 In that day there shall be a fountain opened to the house of David and to the inhabitants of Jerusalem for sin and for uncleanness. 3 And it shall come to pass in that day, says the Lord of hosts, that I will cut off the names of the idols out of the land, and they shall no more be remembered: and also I will cause the prophets and the unclean spirit to pass out of the land. 9 And I will bring the third part through the fire, and will refine them as silver is refined, and will try them as gold is tried: they shall call on my name, and I will hear them: I will say, It is my people: and they shall say, The Lord is my God.

This could be a headline: <u>144,000 Jewish Witnesses Proclaim the Gospel</u>

Revelation 7:3 "'Do not harm the land or the sea or the trees until we put a seal on the foreheads of the servants of our God.' 4 Then I heard the number of those who were sealed: 144,000 from all the tribes of Israel."

When God has miraculously saved Israel, He is going to baptize 144,000 Israelis with the Holy Spirit to travel the world as His missionaries. That will be 12,000 out of each of the twelve tribes. That should start a really fantastic revival. Some people believe that these will be Christians because "we have been grafted in," but it seems clear to me that these will be Jews who will preach the Gospel around the world. That also gives me hope that the Christians will have been raptured out at this time.

Revelation 7:4 "And I heard the number of them which were sealed: and there were sealed a hundred and forty and four thousand of all the tribes of the children of Israel."

If the Church has been raptured, the 144,000 will be the first to be saved during the Tribulation period, and they will be sealed with God's name on their foreheads until their job is finished. Of course, they will suffer persecution by the Antichrist and False Prophet and will be killed, so the next place that you see them is in heaven with Christ, singing a new song.

Revelation 14:3,4 ....no man could learn that song but the hundred and forty and four thousand, which were redeemed from the earth. 4 These are they which were not defiled with women; for they are virgins. These are they which follow the Lamb wherever he goes. These were redeemed from among men, being the first fruits to God and to the Lamb.

CHAPTER 12

The Third Jewish Temple

Perhaps because of the peace treaty, which will divide the city of Jerusalem, the Jews will begin to build their third temple.

Amos 9:11 "In that day I will raise up the tabernacle of David that is fallen, and repair the breaches thereof; and I will raise up his ruins, and I will build it as in the days of old"

Immediately after the Gog, Magog prophecy in 38 and 39, Ezekiel 40 describes the new temple to the last detail. So it will be built, and sacrifices will be offered on the altar there, but in the middle of the seven years of Tribulation, the Antichrist will stop the temple sacrifices.

Daniel 9: 27 "... In the middle of the 'seven' he will put an end to sacrifice and offering. And at the temple he will set up an abomination that causes desolation, until the end that is decreed is poured out on him."

Jesus called it the abomination of **desolation** in Matthew 24:15.

If the Antichrist causes the sacrifice to cease in the middle of the seven years, there must be a temple in which sacrifices have been made. If a temple is to be built according to Daniel 9, using the specification of Ezekiel 40, what happened to the Dome of the Rock, which is on the site of Solomon's temple? The Dome of the Rock and the Al-Aksa Mosques, both Muslim holy sites, stand on the Temple Mount. The destruction of either of these would begin another war, unless they had been destroyed by

God during the Gog/Magog war. The earthquake that is predicted for that time when Russia attacks Israel could easily destroy either or both of the Muslim mosques.

Ezekiel 36:2 "Thus says the Lord God; Because the enemy has said against you, Aha, even the ancient high places are ours in possession……..

Possibly the Dome of the Rock will still be standing and because of the division of Jerusalem, the Temple will be built beside it.

The Temple Institute in Jerusalem was founded by Rabbi Yisrael Ariel in 1987. Its ultimate goal is the re-building of the Third Temple on Mount Moriah, the Temple Mount, in Jerusalem. The Institute has now recreated all the vessels and utensils that are required for the building of the temple and resumption of temple worship. In 2013 a new Ark of the Covenant was completed and is now on display in the Temple Institute.

CHAPTER 13

A New World Order

Paul-Henri Spaak, former Belgian Prime Minister and President of the Consultative Assembly of the Council of Europe nearly 50 years ago, said, "We do not want another committee. We have too many already. What we want is a man of sufficient stature to hold the allegiance of all people and to lift us out of the economic morass in which we are sinking. Send us such a man, and be he God or the devil, we will receive him."

The European Union, which began as the European Economic Community signed the "Treaty of Rome" in 1957, and countries started giving up their national sovereignty in order to join it. According to the Bible, this union will not last but it will exist long enough for a world leader to rise who will destroy three of the European countries. It is not the ten nation world government but the people involved in it have drawn up a plan to divide the world into 10 regions.

Pretty soon, if our country does not become more independent of Arab oil and Chinese money, the Chinese, the Arabs, the "Club of Rome", or the United Nations will force the 247 nations of the world into ten regions, governed by one man. That is the "One World Government" that the Bible talks about in Revelation 13 and Daniel 7. The people behind this plan have an agenda that will completely destroy the U.S. economy so that when the world leaders call in our debts, we will have no recourse except to agree with whatever they say.

IF Christians begin praying and standing up for what is right, their agenda could possibly be derailed for a little while, but even though some government leaders want to wash their hands of this total take-over, others are completely involved in it and I don't think they can be stopped, except by God. I really believe that most of our presidents and high government officials have been in an alliance with the powerful people who are part of the Trilateral Commission, the Bilderbergers, the Council on Foreign Relations, and of course, the United Nations and its security council, They are the financial powers who are behind the scenes, manipulating world events.

CHAPTER 14

The Antichrist

The Antichrist, who is he? Where will he be? How will the world recognize him?

Daniel describes him and what he will do.

Daniel 7:24 The ten horns are ten kings (leaders of 10 world areas*) who will come from this kingdom. After them another king (the Antichrist) will arise, different from the earlier ones; he will subdue three kings. 25 He will speak against the Most High (God) and oppress his holy people (the Jews) and try to change the set times and the laws. The holy people will be delivered into his hands for a time, times and half a time (3 ½ years.)*

Later Daniel exposes more about the Antichrist.

Daniel 8:9-11 "And out of one of them (the countries of the Revived Roman Empire,) came forth another horn, (the Antichrist,) which started small but grew in power to the south, and to the east, and toward the Beautiful Land (Israel.) **10** *It grew, (Satan, embodied in the Antichrist,) until it reached the host of the heavens; and it threw some of the starry host down to the earth and trampled on them.* **11** *It set itself up to be as great as the commander of the army of the Lord; it took away the daily sacrifice from the Lord, and his sanctuary was thrown down.*

Daniel 8 tells more about his character and activities.

Daniel 8:23-25 " In the latter part of their reign, when rebels have become completely wicked, a fierce-looking king, (again, the Antichrist,) a master of intrigue, will arise. 24 He will become very strong, but not by his own power. (He will be using Satan's power,) He will cause astounding devastation and will succeed in whatever he does. He will destroy those who are mighty, the holy people. 25 He will cause deceit to prosper, and he will consider himself superior. When they feel secure, (He will negotiate for and claim to be able to bring peace,) he will destroy many and take his stand against the Prince of princes (Jesus). Yet he will be destroyed, but not by human power.

He tells us about the peace treaty that the Antichrist will negotiate.

Daniel 9:27 He will confirm a covenant with many for one 'seven.' In the middle of the 'seven' he will put an end to sacrifice and offering. And at the temple he will set up an abomination that causes desolation, until the end that is decreed is poured out on him.

Daniel 11 finally tells us what kind of person he will be.

Daniel 11:36 " The king (again, the Antichrist,) will do as he pleases. He will exalt and magnify himself above every god and will say unheard-of-things against the God of gods. He will be successful until the time of wrath (the Great Tribulation) is completed, for what has been determined must take place. 37 He will show no regard for the god of his ancestors or for the one desired by women, nor will he regard any god, but will exalt himself above them all. 38 Instead of them, he will honor a god of fortresses; a god unknown to his ancestors he will honor with gold and silver, with precious stones and costly gifts. 39 He will attack the mightiest fortresses with the help of a foreign god and will greatly honor those who acknowledge him. He will make them rulers over many people and will distribute the land at a price."

The Antichrist will have a fierce countenance, will be a master of intrigue, will cause deceit to prosper, will succeed in whatever he does and will cause astounding devastation. He will negotiate a seven-year peace treaty, will stop the temple sacrifices and destroy the holy people. He will even fight against Jesus.

The Antichrist is also described in Revelation.

*Revelation 13: 1 "The dragon (Satan) stood on the shore of the sea, (*the people?) *And I saw a beast (*the one-world government? The Antichrist?*) coming up out of the sea. It had ten horns* (ten kingdoms) *and seven heads,* (ten nations minus the three that he defeats?) *with ten crowns on its horns (* ten kings?*) and on each head a blasphemous name . 2 The beast I saw resembled a leopard, (*Germany?*) but had feet like those of a bear,* (Russia?) *and a mouth like that of a lion (*England? English language?) *The dragon* (Satan) *gave the beast his power and his throne and great authority. 3 One of the heads of the beast seemed to have had a fatal wound, but the fatal wound had been healed. The whole world was filled with wonder and followed the beast. 4 People worshiped the dragon because he had given authority to the beast, and they also worshiped the beast and asked, "Who is like the beast? Who can wage war against it?" 5 The beast was given a mouth to utter proud words and blasphemies; and to exercise his authority forty-two months (* 3 ½ years). *6 It opened its mouth to blaspheme God, and to slander his name, and his dwelling place and those who live in heaven. 7 It was given power to wage war against God's holy people and to conquer them. And it was given authority over every tribe, people, language and nation,* (One-world government.) *8 All inhabitants of the earth will worship the beast—all whose names have not been written in the Lamb's book of life, the Lamb* (Jesus) *who was slain from the creation of the world.*

2 Thessalonians 2:4 says that *"He displays himself as God."*

From the scriptures, we see ten descriptive marks of the Antichrist:

1. He will arise out of the fourth beast which was the Revived Roman Empire.
2. He will arise among the 10 horns/division of the Revived Roman Empire.
3. As he arises, he will destroy 3 kingdoms of the Revived Roman Empire.
4. He will begin little but become stronger than the others.

5. He will be different from the others.

6. He will have eyes like the eyes of man and speak great words of blasphemy against the Most High.

7. He will exalt himself as God.

8. He will try to change times and laws.

9. 9. He will persecute the saints.

10.10. He will reign for three and a half years.

2 Thessalonians 2:8-10 "And then the lawless one (the Antichrist) *will be revealed, whom the Lord Jesus will overthrow with the breath of his mouth and destroy by the splendor of his coming. The coming of the lawless one will be in accordance with how Satan works. He will use all sorts of displays of power through signs and wonders that serve the lie, and all the ways that wickedness deceives those who are perishing."*

What will happen to him?

Daniel 11:40 "At the time of the end, the king of the South (Africa?Egypt?) *will engage him in battle, and the king of the North* (Russia?) *will storm out against him with chariots and cavalry and a great fleet of ships. He will invade many countries and sweep through them like a flood. 41 He will also invade the Beautiful Land,* (Israel*) and the leaders of Ammon* (Jordan*?) will be delivered from his hand. 42 He will extend his power over many countries; Egypt will not escape. 43 He will gain control of the treasures of gold and silver and all the riches of Egypt, with the Libyans and Cushites in submission. 4 But reports from the east and the north will alarm him, and he will set out in a great rage to destroy and annihilate many. 45 He will pitch his royal tents between the seas at the beautiful holy mountain. (*Jerusalem*) Yet he will come to his end and no one will help him."*

Daniel 7:11 "Then I continued to watch because of the boastful words the horn (the Antichrist*) was speaking. I kept looking until the beast was slain and its body destroyed and thrown into the blazing fire."*

We know what will eventually happen to him, but the Antichrist, by Satanic power, will have complete control over the entire world for three and a half years. He will also have an accomplice to help with the deception by displays of supernatural signs and wonders.

What does the Pope have to do with it?

CHAPTER 15

The False Prophet

The False Prophet comes as a lamb (like Christ) but speaks like Satan. He comes out of the earth, (speaking of the masses of people who accept him,) and is given great authority by the Antichrist. He will have demonic power so that he can perform great signs even showing fire come down from heaven as Elijah did on Mt. Carmel. The inhabitants of the earth will be deceived so that when he orders an image of the beast to be created and then makes it seem to come alive, all bow down to the image. If they do not worship the beast, they will be killed.

Revelation 13: 11. "Then I saw a second beast, coming out of the earth. It had two horns like a lamb, but it spoke like a dragon. 12 It exercised all the authority of the first beast on its behalf, and made the earth and its inhabitants worship the first beast whose fatal wound had been healed. 13 And it performed great signs even causing fire to come down from heaven to the earth in full view of the people 14 Because of the signs it was given power to perform on behalf of the first beast, it deceived the inhabitants of the earth. It ordered them to set up an image in honor of the beast who was wounded by the sword and yet lived. 15 The second beast was given power to give breath to the image of the first beast, so that the image could speak and cause all who refused to worship the image to be killed.

What if the image of the beast is on interactive television? Computers? Cell phones? Giving life to the image would not be hard on these devices. Question: How will the antichrist know if someone does not worship him?

Matthew 8:28-32, is the story of Jesus driving demons out of the Gadarene maniacs and it shows us about demons. 1. Demons require a physical object through which to operate. 2. They indwell men and can speak through them. 3. They are able to create great violence. 4. They do not seem to have the ability to choose their physical abode, but can get in anything living if there is an opening.

Revelation 12:9 says that the great dragon (Satan) is thrown down in the middle of the tribulation. His abode will be the body of the Antichrist. But, the demonic spirits that are thrown down with him will need homes.

Revelation 16:13 "Then I saw three impure spirits that looked like frogs; they came out of the mouth of the dragon, out of the mouth of the beast and out of the mouth of the false prophet. 14 They are demonic spirits that perform signs, and they go out to the kings of the whole world, to gather them for the battle on the great day of God Almighty."

Who is the False Prophet? Who will attempt and be successful in drawing all religions together? Who controls a large majority of religious people now? Who is willing to compromise and say that Allah and God are the same? Who is the head of the Babylonian religion that is described in Revelation?

Pope Francis has made the news recently because of some meetings with Islamic religious leaders. One even came to the Vatican. He is also encouraging all Christian denominations to join with the Catholic Church to promote unity.

The pope of the Catholic Church even believes that he has authority in Jerusalem. The Catholic Church has long wanted control over part of the area on Mt. Zion in order to turn it into an international religious center for Catholics. However, the agreements to give him a seat in Jerusalem are not being widely reported.

Journalist Joel Bainerman, a well-known commentator on Israeli affairs, claims, "The end goal of the Vatican is to seize control of the Old City of Jerusalem out of the clutches of the State of Israel. To that end they have a secret agreement with Israel which obliges Israel to respect the 'extraterritorial' claim to their physical presence in the city. In short, we have accepted the Vatican's rights to have little Vatican sovereign embassies throughout our eternal capital of Jerusalem. That same Vatican has committed itself, in public and in a written agreement, to ensure that the Palestinians have sovereignty in the Old City of Jerusalem."

Op-Ed: Exclusive: A Seat for the Pope at King David's Tomb Giulio Meotti, 01/02/13

"An historic agreement has been drafted between Israel and the Vatican. The Israeli authorities have granted the Pope an official seat in the room where the Last Supper is believed to have taken place, on Mount Zion in Jerusalem, and where David and Solomon, Jewish kings of Judea, are considered by some researchers, to also be buried."

Will one of the popes become the False Prophet? Who is the pope that will insist on having some part of Jerusalem? Does the pope have that kind of power? Will he be given even more power by the Antichrist?

CHAPTER 16

The Mark Of The Beast

There has long been a move toward a "One-World Government", a world currency, and a world religion. Begun in secret, it has now become accepted and acceptable even by Christians. None of this scripture in Revelation seems impossible in the day in which we live. With technology taking us where we do not want to go, we now realize that we are living in the days when this can happen.

Revelation 13:16-18 "And he, (the second beast/ false prophet,) *causes all, both small and great, rich and poor, free and slave, to receive a mark in their right hand, or in their foreheads: and that no man might buy or sell, except he that had the mark, or the name of the beast, or the number of his name. Here is wisdom. Let him that understands count the number of the beast: for it is the number of a man; and his number is six hundred threescore and six."*

There is a computer system that can count and store information on every person in the world.

Britain's *The Guardian* newspaper summarized the capabilities of the ECHELON system as follows:

"A global network of electronic spy stations that can eavesdrop on telephones, faxes and computers. It can even track bank accounts. This information is stored in Echelon computers, which can keep millions of records on individuals. Officially, however, Echelon doesn't exist."

There is a microchip that will make it possible to control every person.

"Implanted computer chips for humans have been approved by the FDA."
October 5, 2012 by David Cornell

"Will Microchip Implants in Humans Become Mandatory?"
Written by Selwyn Duke Saturday, 03 May 2014

The microchip is already being implanted in animals and in some people. The chip in your GPS, in your car, in your cell phone, and in your credit card ostensibly to protect from terrorism or identity theft are preparing people to accept a mark in their hand or their forehead. Tattoos have become so prevalent that it will make it easy to accept a special identification tattoo on your hand or forehead, especially if it will make everything more convenient. The cashless society is almost here.

In 2012, the Bilderbergers met in Chantilly, Virginia and on their agenda was a plan to microchip every individual in America. They will initiate the threat of terrorism to such an extreme that when the authorities say it is essential to fight terrorism, people will agree. People think nothing of giving up their privacy and their freedom to retain their safety and comfort. The national ID is the first step in this direction. In the name of safety after 9/11, we have willingly let the government monitor everything we do.

In 2005, our Congress passed a law called the REAL ID Act, a national ID database, negating the Fourth Amendment which guarantees Americans the right to control what others see of their private information. It is a federally-controlled ID card which can be used for any "official purpose" and requires biometric information, including fingerprints or eye scans. Some states have refused to comply but on January 22, 2018, if your state has not complied, you may not be able to board an airplane or enter a federal building.

Then, on December 8, 2016, the House passed HR 4919, a bill to microchip US citizens. It would allow the US attorney general to establish the use of tracking devices to find "individuals with forms of dementia or children with disabilities." That probably sounds reasonable to some people, until you realize that there are no restrictions on the inclusion of other individuals. Whomever the government decides should be tracked would be tracked. Giving a government who doesn't read the bills before they vote on them, the ability to microchip whomever they please, doesn't give me a secure feeling. "Big Brother" is here!

There are satellites that can allow every part of the world to be viewed.

Satellite-Surveillance Program to Begin Despite Privacy Concerns

By **SIOBHAN GORMAN** Updated Oct. 1, 2008 12:01 a.m. ET

WASHINGTON – "The Department of Homeland Security will proceed with the first phase of a controversial satellite-surveillance program, even though an independent review found the department hasn't yet ensured the program will comply with privacy laws. "

There are mind-control instruments being developed which are extremely dangerous and should be outlawed by every government but are being kept a secret and may be used against us.

"The US military is supposed to be prohibited by law from targeting US citizens with PSYOPS within US borders under Executive Order S-1233, DOD directive S-3321.1 and National Security Directive 120. Of course there's no one to police that especially since Psyops, by their very nature, are difficult to prove. This is particularly so where the secret weapons discussed on this web site are employed. Also nothing stops agencies, US or allied, from doing that dirty work and hiding it under the National Security carpet. Nonetheless, public discussion of these Psyops crimes is beginning. See Dr. Keith Ablow, psychiatrist of Fox News."

"The European Parliament passed a 'Resolution on the Environment, Security and Foreign Policy –A4-0005/99, January 28th, 1999' which called for 'An international convention introducing a global ban on ALL development and deployment of weapons which might enable any form of manipulation of human beings'... 'It is our conviction that this ban cannot be implemented without the global pressure of the informed general public on governments. Our major objective is to get across to the general public the real threat which these weapons represent for human rights and democracy and to apply pressure on the governments and the parliaments around the world to enact legislation which would prohibit the use of these devices to both government AND private organizations as well as individuals'. (Plenary sessions/European Parliament. 1999)."

The False Prophet will require a two-fold test:

1. You must worship the image of the beast or be killed.

2. You must take the mark of the beast or be unable to buy or sell.

Bowing to the Antichrist and allowing a certain mark to be placed in you or on you will condemn you to the wrath of God, to be tormented with fire and brimstone forever. No matter what happens, remember that your beheading is only for a second in the face of eternity. Do not be sorrowful at the death of a loved one who dies in the Lord, for they will not have to go through this. It will be so hard to let loved ones die of starvation or torture, but it will quickly be over and we can spend eternity in Heaven.

Revelation 3:10 calls it the hour of testing. 1 Peter 1:7 refers to testing by fire. 1 Peter 4:12 calls it the fiery ordeal. 1 Timothy 4:1 talks about some in the compromising church falling. Revelation 14:11,12 talks about the perseverance of the saints.

True believers who accept Christ during the Tribulation will refuse to worship and take the mark but will be persecuted and beheaded. Members of the compromising and dead churches will likely take the mark to survive and avoid persecution, only to face an eternity in Hell and separation from God

CHAPTER 17

The Tribulation Period

The seals in Revelation 6 are an overview of the Tribulation period. We know this because of the heavenly disasters reported in verses 12-14.

All over the world, the saints of God are even now enduring great persecution, just as Jesus said, and the closer to His Second Coming, the more intense will be the persecution.

Matthew 24: 9 "Then shall they deliver you up to tribulation and shall kill you: and you shall be hated of all nations for my name's sake."

Rev. 6:9-10 "And when he had opened the fifth seal, I saw under the altar the souls of them that were slain for the word of God, and for the testimony which they held: And they cried with a loud voice, saying, How long, O Lord, holy and true, dost thou not judge and avenge our blood on them that dwell on the earth? And white robes were given unto every one of them; and it was said unto them, that they should rest yet for a little season, until their fellow servants also and their brethren, that should be killed as they were, should be fulfilled."

People have been killing one another since the beginning of time, (Cain and Abel,) but this scripture refers to those that were slain for the Word of God, and for their testimony, so they are followers of God. The Romans, Jews, Catholic Church, the Crusaders, the Church of England and the Nazis killed many followers of God. The Communist governments,

Muslims, and various governments have killed and are killing God's followers by the millions. So there are souls already in Heaven crying, "How long until you avenge our blood?"

The tribulation period will begin when the Antichrist from the Revived Roman Empire, (Europe,) appears as one of the main negotiators of a peace treaty between the Palestinians and Israel. Daniel 9:27 The Peace Treaty will divide Jerusalem. The Rapture of the Christians may occur about this time but different scriptures seem to indicate different times for the church to be taken out of the world. So no one knows for certain.

According to Ezekiel, Russia and her Muslim allies will attack Israel and God will miraculously save Israel and destroy the Russian army and their allies with storms, hail, fire and brimstone. (Ezekiel 38) As a result, Israel will accept Jesus as the Messiah. *(Ezekiel 39:22) "From that day forward the people of Israel will know that I am the Lord their God."*

Then 144,000 Jews will take the message of Jesus to the world. (Revelation 7) The Temple will be built and the Jews will begin sacrificing in it. (Ezekiel 40)

The Antichrist will become the world leader. Revelation 13:7 "..... *And it* (the Antichrist,) *was given authority over every tribe, people, language and nation."*

A False Prophet will rise up in support of the Antichrist. *Revelation 13:12 "It exercised all the authority of the first beast on its behalf and made the earth and its inhabitants worship the first beast."* Muslims/ Catholics/ other religions/ false Christians will join together to make up a One World Religion and to stop the Messianic Jews from preaching Christ.

The tribulation period begins with what are called "Trumpet Judgments."

1. First Trumpet: Hail storms and fires will burn up 1/3 of trees and all the grass.

Revelation 8:7 7 The first angel sounded, and there followed hail and fire mingled with blood, and they were cast upon the earth: and the third part of trees was burnt up, and all green grass was burnt up.

Many scriptures describe the world-wide fires that will burn at that time.

Ezekiel 20:47

47 And say to the forest of the south, Hear the word of the LORD; This is what the Lord GOD says; Behold, I will kindle a fire in you, and it shall devour every green tree in you, and every dry tree: the flaming flame shall not be quenched, and all faces from the south to the north shall be burned in it.

Joel 2:3,30

3 A fire devours before them; and behind them a flame burns: the land is as the garden of Eden before them, and behind them a desolate wilderness; yes, nothing shall escape them. 30 And I will show wonders in the heavens and in the earth, blood, and fire, and pillars of smoke. Obadiah 1:18 Jacob will be a fire and Joseph a flame; Esau will be stubble, and they will set him on fire and destroy him. There will be no survivors from Esau." The Lord has spoken.

Zephaniah 1:18

18 Neither their silver nor their gold shall be able to deliver them in ; but the whole land shall be devoured by the fire of his jealousy: for he shall make even a speedy riddance of all them that dwell in the land.

Malachi 4:1 1

For, behold, the day cometh, that shall burn as an oven; and all the proud, yea, and all that do wickedly, shall be stubble: and the day that cometh shall burn them up, saith the LORD of hosts, that it shall leave them neither root nor branch.

Psalms 97:3

A fire goes before him, and burns up his enemies round about.

Isaiah 66:15 For, behold, the LORD will come with fire, and with his chariots like a whirlwind, to render his anger with fury, and his rebuke with flames of fire.

16 For by fire and by his sword will the LORD plead with all flesh: and the slain of the LORD shall be many.

Fire, smoke and brimstone will spout out of the mouths of armored tanks, artillery or bombs to kill a third of men. (A nuclear battle?)

Revelation 9:18 By these three was the third part of men killed, by the fire, and by the smoke, and by the brimstone, which issued out of their mouths.

2. Second Trumpet: A burning mountain, (perhaps a volcano?) will destroy a third of all the creatures in the sea and a third of all the ships. As mentioned before, many volcanoes world-wide are beginning to rumble.

Revelation 8:8 The second angel sounded his trumpet, and something like a huge mountain, all ablaze, was thrown into the sea. A third of the sea turned into blood, a third of the living creatures in the sea died, and a third of the ships were destroyed.

3. Third Trumpet: A burning star falling from the sky makes 1/3 of the waters bitter.

Revelation 8:10 The third angel sounded his trumpet, and a great star, blazing like a torch, fell from the sky on a third of the rivers and on the springs of water—11 the name of the star is Wormwood. A third of the waters turned bitter, and many people died from the waters that had become bitter.

In 1986, the Chernobyl nuclear plant in Ukraine blew up and destroyed all the life and waters in that area. Chernobyl in Russian means wormwood. A pre-cursor of things to come?

4. Fourth Trumpet: One third of sun, moon, and stars will be darkened. (When the volcano erupted over Europe, no airplanes could fly because of the smoke obstructing vision.)

Revelation 8:12 The fourth angel sounded his trumpet, and a third of the sun was struck, a third of the moon, and a third of the stars, so that a third of them turned dark. A third of the day was without light, and also a third of the night.

5. Fifth Trumpet: Smoke from the Abyss will also be darkening the skies and locusts which have stings like scorpions will be released from the Abyss to torment anyone without God's seal on their foreheads.

Revelation 9:1 The fifth angel sounded his trumpet, and I saw a star that had fallen from the sky to the earth. The star was given the key to the shaft of the Abyss. 2 When he opened the Abyss, smoke rose from it like the smoke from a gigantic furnace. The sun and sky were darkened by the smoke from the Abyss. 3 And out of the smoke locusts came down on the earth and were given power like that of scorpions of the earth.

The locusts John described looked like horses prepared for battle, having crowns of gold, faces like men, hair like women's, teeth like lions, breastplates of iron. They sounded like chariots, had tails like scorpions, and were given power for five months. The king over them is called Abaddon, (the Destroyer.) Revelation. 9:7-11

Could these be real demons or helicopters or drones?

To summarize, when the catastrophes begin and a seven-year peace treaty is signed, the anti-Christ will appear. Then the false prophet will show great signs and wonders to get people to believe that the antichrist is the real Messiah and will be so convincing that they will fool the people, even the elect, if it were possible.

In the middle of the seven years, the Antichrist will stand in the temple, proclaiming himself God. So the temple in Jerusalem must be built before that time. That makes us ask the question, "What about the 'Dome of the Rock' that stands where the temple should be built? What happens to it?

Then the great tribulation starts. You definitely don't want to be here for that. The first three and a half years will be terrible but the last three and a half will be worse than anyone can imagine. I started to say, "indescribable," but the Bible actually describes the horrors.

CHAPTER 18

The Great Tribulation

At the mid-point of the seven-year tribulation period, the Antichrist will be seated in the temple in Jerusalem, declaring that he is God. It is called, "The Abomination of Desolation," and will be the introduction of the "Great Tribulation," and it is foretold by Paul, Daniel and Jesus.

2 Thess. 2:1-3 "...concerning the coming of our Lord Jesus Christ, and concerning our gathering together unto him, ... 3 Let no man deceive you by any means; for that day shall not come, except there be a falling away first, and that man of sin be revealed, the son of perdition; 4 who opposes and exalts himself above all that is called God, or that is worshiped; so that he as God sits in the temple of God, showing himself that he is God."

Daniel 9:27 "....In the middle of the 'seven' (the seven year peace agreement) *he* (the Antichrist,) *will put an end to sacrifice and offering* (in the temple.) *And at the temple he will set up an abomination that causes desolation, until the end that is decreed is poured out on him."*

Matthew 24 "When you therefore see the ABOMINATION OF DESOLATION, spoken of by Daniel the prophet, stand in the holy place, (whoso reads, let him understand:) then let them which be in Judea flee into the mountains: let him which is on the housetop not come down to take anything out of his house: neither let him which is in the field return back to take his clothes. And woe unto them that are pregnant and to them who are nursing babies in those days!"

"But pray that your flight is not in the winter, nor on the Sabbath day; ***for then shall be great tribulation, such as was not since the beginning of the world to this time, no, nor ever shall be.*** *And except those days should be shortened, there should no flesh be saved: but for the elect's sake those days shall be shortened."*

The Beast, (the Antichrist,) will take control of the entire world. The world will be divided into ten geographical areas. He will blaspheme God, will make war with the saints and will overcome them until Jesus returns with His army from Heaven. He will be killed but will be brought back to life, (Satan always tries to imitate Christ,) with Satan himself controlling his body.

Luke 10:18 "He (Jesus) replied, 'I saw Satan fall like lightning from heaven."

Just an interesting side note: **"Lightning Strikes One World Trade Center Twice"** | 05/23/14

One World Trade Center (also known as the **Freedom Tower**,) is the main building of the rebuilt World Trade Center complex in Lower Manhattan, New York City. It is the tallest building in the Western Hemisphere, and the sixth-tallest in the world. On March 30, 2009, the Port Authority of New York and New Jersey(PANYNJ) confirmed that the building would be officially known by its legal name of "One World Trade Center", rather than its colloquial name of "Freedom Tower". That goes along with the fact that we are in the era of the

"One World Government"

An image of the Beast will be constructed and the False Prophet will make the image come alive. He will demand that all worship it. Everyone will be commanded to bow down to Satan and will be required to take the mark of the Beast in order to buy or sell. There will be no currency. Everything will be done automatically via the identity chip in the head or hand.

Revelation 13:15 "*The second beast....16 forced all people, great and small, rich and poor, free and slave, to receive a mark on their right hands or on their foreheads, 17 so that they could not buy or sell unless they had the mark...*"

The 144,000 Jewish witnesses who have been traveling the world witnessing that Jesus is the Messiah, will be put to death. But never leaving Himself without a witness, God will send an angel to preach the Gospel.

Revelation 14:6 "And I saw another angel fly in the midst of heaven, having the everlasting gospel to preach to them that dwell on the earth, and to every nation, and tribe, and tongue, and people."

There will be two witnesses who stop it from raining for 31/2 years. The world will see them killed in Jerusalem, be celebrating their deaths as they lie in the streets, and on the third day, watch them, via television, be raised up into Heaven. Revelation 11:12 ".......And they went up to heaven in a cloud, while their enemies looked on. 13 At that very hour there was a severe earthquake and a tenth of the city collapsed. Seven thousand people were killed in the earthquake, and the survivors were terrified and gave glory to the God of heaven."

A second angel will announce the destruction of Babylon and a third angel will warn everyone about taking the mark or worshipping the beast. Revelation 14:9 "....'If anyone worships the beast and its image and receives its mark on their forehead or on their hand, they, too, will drink the wine of God's fury,.....They will be tormented with burning sulfur ....forever and ever.'"

The Woman (Israel) will flee to the desert for 31/2 years because the Gentiles will take over Jerusalem for that time. *Revelation 1:6 "The woman* (Israel*) fled into the wilderness to a place prepared for her by God, where she might be taken care of for 1,260 days.". Revelation 11:2 ".....it (the outer courts of the temple) has been given to the Gentiles. They will trample on the holy city for 42 months."*

The last part of tribulation, God 's Wrath, includes the seven bowl judgments in Revelation 16:

1.Anyone who does not have God's seal on their forehead will have painful sores all over their bodies.

2. The sea will turn to blood and everything in the sea will be destroyed.

3. The rivers will turn to blood.

4. The sun will become so hot that it will scorch men.

5. The seat where the Beast is headquartered will be turned to darkness and pain.

6. At the River Euphrates the angels will be loosed, the river will be dried up, the Kings of the East and their 200 million-man armies will march across. (There are many armies in the area of the Euphrates River already. The Chinese are building a road toward it. There is a dam in Turkey that controls it.) There will be a battle (Armageddon) in and around Jerusalem that fills the country of Israel with blood up to the horses' bridles and 1/3 of men will be slain at the Battle of Armageddon.

7. There will be a great earthquake, in which Jerusalem will be separated into three parts. All the cities of all the nations will be destroyed. One-hundred-pound hailstones will fall on people. And Babylon will be destroyed.

CHAPTER 19

Which Babylon?

Revelation 16:19 "God remembered Babylon the Great and gave her the cup filled with the wine of the fury of his wrath."

Who is Babylon the Great? Is it ancient Babylon in Iraq that Saddam Hussein tried to rebuild? Is it Jerusalem? Is it America? Is it Rome? Let's see if we can decipher and solve the mystery of Babylon.

Jeremiah 51:7 "Babylon has been a golden cup in the Lord's hand that made all the earth drunken: the nations have drunk of her wine; therefore the nations are mad."

The beginning of idol worship started with the construction of the Tower of Bab-El, (which meant the gate of God,) by Nimrod, a descendant of Ham, as man's attempt to be on the same level with God. It was halted when God confused the languages and the people were scattered. But as they spread throughout the whole earth, so did the idol worship and sexual practices that became the basis of the Babylonian mystery-religion. Because Satan often deceives by imitating the truth of God, he introduced the mother and child worship long before the virgin birth of Christ, so that the people would not know the true Savior when He came.

In this pagan deception, Semiramis bore a son whom she declared was miraculously conceived, and when she presented him to the people, he was hailed as the promised deliverer. This was Tammuz, whose worship

Ezekiel protested against in the days of the Babylonian captivity. The image of the queen of heaven with the babe in her arms was seen everywhere, though with different names.

Although Babylon as a city had been destroyed long before the birth of Christ, the Babylonian religion continued as the Etruscan Mysteries and their worship was celebrated with the most disgusting and immoral practices. Some of the other mysteries of this Mystery-Babylon were the doctrines of purgatory and praying for the dead, salvation by sprinkling with holy water, the offering of round cakes to the queen of heaven, sins being absolved by priests, and dedication of virgins to the gods (prostitution).

There was a 40 - day season of weeping for Tammuz (Lent?) before the festival of Ishtar (Easter?) who was said to have received her son, Tammuz, back from the dead. His resurrection was depicted by a sacred egg and his birth was celebrated by the evergreen, (the Christmas tree?) The sign of the cross was sacred to Tammuz, as the first letter of his name. All of these idolatrous practices were promulgated into religions and cults throughout the ancient world long before Jesus was born. Rome eventually became the headquarters of Babylonianism, where the chief priests wore mitres shaped like the head of a fish, in honor of Dagon, the fish-god. You will often see these on the heads of the cardinals at the Vatican.

Revelation 17:1 "One of the seven angels who had the seven bowls came and said to me, 'Come, I will show you the punishment of the great prostitute, who sits by many waters. 2 With her the kings of the earth committed adultery, and the inhabitants of the earth were intoxicated with the wine of her adulteries.'"

Revelation 17:3 "Then the angel carried me away in the Spirit into a wilderness. There I saw a woman sitting on a scarlet beast that was covered with blasphemous names and had seven heads and ten horns......5 The name written on her forehead was a mystery: BABYLON THE GREAT THE MOTHER OF PROSTITUTES AND OF THE ABOMINATIONS OF THE

EARTH. 6 I saw that the woman was drunk with the blood of God's holy people, the blood of those who bore testimony to Jesus.."

The woman, Mystery Babylon could be the Babylon of the past in Iraq. It could be Jerusalem or Rome, both of which at the time John was writing were sometimes referred to as Babylon. Or it could be a future Babylon, possibly America.

But America has never persecuted God's people. The old Babylon, in the country that is now Iraq, wasn't around when Jesus' followers were persecuted and slain. Jerusalem does not fit the rest of the description. So, all roads lead to Rome, the seat of the church, mixing with the Babylonian religion, which fits exactly the description of Mystery Babylon. The woman, drunk with the blood of God's holy people who bore testimony to Jesus, had to be Rome, which was persecuting Jesus' followers at that time and would continue the persecution of true followers of Christ throughout the centuries.

Revelation 17:8 The beast, which you saw once was, now is not, and yet will come up out of the Abyss and go to its destruction. The inhabitants of the earth whose names have not been written in the book of life from the creation of the world will be astonished when they see the beast, because it once was, now is not, and yet will come.

Who is the beast that, "once was, now is not, and yet will come up out of the Abyss that the woman, Mystery Babylon, (Catholicism) sits on?

Revelation 17:9 This calls for a mind with wisdom. The seven heads are seven hills on which the woman sits.

The city of Rome is built on seven hills. So the woman, Mystery Babylon, sits on the seven hills of Rome. It is Vatican City, the headquarters of the Catholic Church.

In 1 Peter 5:13, when Peter writes, "the chosen one at Babylon," Peter was at Rome, where he was crucified and Babylon was a code name for Rome.

Revelation 17:10 *"They are also seven kings."* (The seven hills also represent seven Roman kings.*) "Five have fallen, one is,* (Augustus Caesar?) *the other has not yet come, but when he does come,* (the seventh king?*) he must remain for only a little while."* (Rome's era as a monarchy ended in 509 B.C. with the overthrow of its seventh king, Lucius Tarquinius Superbus.) *11 The beast (the Antichrist) who once was, and now is not, is an eighth king. He belongs to the seven (Roman kings,) and is going to his destruction."*

So, the eighth king is the beast who once was, and now is not. If he belongs to the seven, he must be the one who rules over or is part of the Revived Roman Empire. The prostitute, Babylon, the religion headquartered in Rome, sits on the beast. So it will evidently be supported at first by the Antichrist.

15 The waters you saw, where the prostitute (the World Church,) *sits, are peoples, multitudes, nations and languages. 16 The beast* (the Antichrist,) *and the ten horns* (the rulers of ten kingdoms,) *you saw will hate the prostitute,* (the World Church.) *They will bring her to ruin and leave her naked; they will eat her flesh and burn her with fire… (*This could be caused by volcanoes in the area, which are beginning to rumble and causing earthquakes as of this writing or it could be the result of nuclear warheads or ISIS which is already threatening to destroy Rome.) *18 The woman you saw is the great city that rules over the kings of the earth.* (This again makes it clear that we are talking about Rome in this description of Babylon because Rome ruled over the known world at that time.)

18:2 With a mighty voice he (the angel) shouted: "Fallen! Fallen is Babylon the Great! She has become a dwelling for demons and a haunt for every impure spirit, a haunt for every unclean bird, a haunt for every unclean and detestable animal. 3 For all the nations have drunk the maddening wine of her adulteries. The kings of the earth committed adultery with her, and the merchants of the earth grew rich from her excessive luxuries. (I admit this description could be of New York City and America but the rest of it so fits the Catholic Church, which has been in bed with the kings of the earth since its conception, that I still think it is Roman Catholicism uniting all the religions of the world into a One World Religion.) 8*....in one day her plagues will overtake her: death, mourning and famine. She will be consumed by fire, for mighty is the Lord God who judges her.*

9 When the kings of the earth who committed adultery with her and shared her luxury see the smoke of her burning, they will weep and mourn over her. 11 The merchants of the earth will weep and mourn over her because no one buys their cargoes anymore----cargoes of gold, silver, precious stones and pearls; fine linen, purple, silk and scarlet cloth; every sort of citron wood, and articles of every kind made of ivory, costly wood, bronze, iron and marble; 13 cargoes of cinnamon and spice, of incense, myrrh and frankincense, of wine and olive oil, of fine flour and wheat; cattle and sheep; horses and carriages; and human beings sold as slaves.

15 The merchants who sold these things and gained their wealth from her will stand far off, terrified at her torment. They will weep and mourn 16 and cry out: Woe! Woe to you, great city, dressed in fine linen, purple and scarlet, and glittering with gold, precious stones and pearls! (No churches have ever been arrayed like the Catholic churches and its popes.) *17 In one hour such great wealth has been brought to ruin! Every sea captain, and all who traveled by ship.....will exclaim, 'Was there ever a city like this great city?'*

21 Then a mighty angel picked up a boulder the size of a large millstone and threw it into the sea, and said: 'With such violence the great city of Babylon will be thrown down, never to be found again. 22 The music of harpists and musicians, pipers and trumpeters, will never be heard in you again. No worker of any trade will ever be found in you again. The sound of a millstone will never be heard in you again. 23 The light of a lamp will never shine in you again., The voice of bridegroom and bride will never be heard in you again. Your merchants were the world's important people. By your magic spell all the nations were led astray. 24 In her was found the blood of prophets and of God's holy people, of all who have been slaughtered on the earth."

The destruction of Rome will likely occur around the time that the Antichrist proclaims himself to be God for he would have no use for intercessors and priests if he sees himself as God.

CHAPTER 20

The Two Witnesses

Revelation 11: 1-14

I was given a reed like a measuring rod and was told, "Go and measure the temple of God and the altar, with its worshipers. But exclude the outer court; do not measure it, because it has been given to the Gentiles. They will trample on the holy city for 42 months. (three and a half years.) And I will appoint my two witnesses, and they will prophesy for 1,260 days, (three and a half years,) clothed in sackcloth. They are the two olive trees" and the two lamp stands, and they stand before the Lord of the earth. If anyone tries to harm them, fire comes from their mouths and devours their enemies. This is how anyone who wants to harm them must die. They have power to shut up the heavens so that it will not rain during the time they are prophesying; and they have power to turn the waters into blood and to strike the earth with every kind of plague as often as they want.

Now when they have finished their testimony, the beast (Satan,) that comes up from the Abyss (the subterranean abode of Satan and his demons,) will attack them, and overpower and kill them. Their bodies will lie in the public square of the great city –which is figuratively called Sodom and Egypt—where also their Lord was crucified. (We know Jesus was crucified in Jerusalem.) For three and a half days some from every people, tribe, language and nation will gaze on their bodies and refuse them burial. The inhabitants of the earth will gloat over them and will celebrate by sending each other gifts, because these two prophets had tormented those who live on the earth.

But after the three and a half days the breath of life from God entered them, and they stood on their feet, and terror struck those who saw them. Then they heard a loud voice from heaven saying to them, "Come up here." And they went up to heaven in a cloud, while their enemies looked on.

At that very hour there was a severe earthquake and a tenth of the city collapsed. Seven thousand people were killed in the earthquake, and the survivors were terrified and gave glory to the God of heaven.

The second woe has passed; the third woe is coming soon.

Most people think that these two witnesses will be Moses and Elijah because that is who appeared with Jesus on the Mount of Transfiguration in Luke 9:30. That may be since they will call down fire like Elijah did on Mt. Carmel and there was a drought in his day as there will be in the days of these prophets. They will also turn water into blood and strike the earth with plagues as Moses did, so it is reasonable to think that they will be the two witnesses.

Malachi 4:5 says, "Elijah will come before that great and dreadful day of the Lord comes," but Jesus said that Elijah had already come as John the Baptist, and Luke 1:17 says that John the Baptist was to come in the spirit and power of Elijah. In Matthew 11:13-14, Jesus told the crowds that "He is the Elijah who was to come." So, if he has already come, is he to come again as one of the two witnesses?

Right before the chapter in Revelation about the two witnesses, the apostle John is told, "You must prophesy again about many peoples, nations, languages and kings. So, why couldn't one of those witnesses be John? The other person who is told that they will "stand at the end of the days" is Daniel. Daniel 12:13 But go thou thy way till the end be: for thou shalt rest, and stand in thy lot at the end of the days.

It doesn't really matter who they are, it is just interesting to think about who will come to warn mankind that the end of the age is here.

CHAPTER 21

Armageddon

Zechariah 12:2 Behold, I will make Jerusalem a cup of trembling unto all the people round about, when they shall be in the siege both against Judah and against Jerusalem. 3 And in that day will I make Jerusalem a burdensome stone for all people: all that burden themselves with it shall be cut in pieces, though all the people of the earth be gathered together against it. 4 In that day, says the Lord, I will smite every horse with confusion, and his rider with madness: and I will open mine eyes upon the house of Judah, and will smite every horse of the peoples with blindness. 5 And the governors of Judah shall say in their heart, The inhabitants of Jerusalem shall be my strength in the Lord of hosts their God.

6 In that day I will make the governors of Judah like a firepan in the woodpile and like a torch of fire in a sheaf; and they shall devour all the people round about, on the right hand and on the left: and Jerusalem shall be inhabited again in her own place, even in Jerusalem. 7 The Lord also shall save the tents of Judah first, that the glory of the house of David and the glory of the inhabitants of Jerusalem do not magnify themselves against Judah. 8 In that day the Lord shall defend the inhabitants of Jerusalem; and he that is feeble among them at that day shall be as David; and the house of David shall be as God, as the angel of the Lord before them. 9 And it shall come to pass in that day, that I will seek to destroy all the nations that come against Jerusalem.

There will be a 200 million man army from the east that will march across the dried-up Euphrates River into the Middle East and fight with all the nations against Israel at the valley of Megido.

Revelation 9:12-18

*12 One woe is past; and, behold, there come two woes more hereafter. 13 And the sixth angel sounded, and I heard a voice from the four horns of the golden altar which is before God, 14 Saying to the sixth angel which had the trumpet, Loose the four angels which are bound in the great river Euphrates. 15 And the four angels were loosed, which were prepared for an hour, and a day, and a month, and a year, for to slay the third part of men.(*1/3 of Earths' Population will die.) *16 And the number of the army of the horsemen were two hundred thousand thousand: (*200 million man army from China and the kings of the east*) and I heard the number of them.*

That time might be nearer than we think, if you consider the warnings that have been in some older headlines.

"Russia Warns China Invasion Of Middle East Nearer Than Thought" Mar. 30, 2011 By: Sorcha Faal, and as reported to her Western Subscribers

"According to Minister Serdyukov, the most vital aspect of this new strategic agreement is the allowing by Pakistan for Chinese military forces to begin the "*immediate use*" of the Karakoram Highway which will allow China's massive ground forces direct access to the Middle East and into direct confrontation with the West."

REVELATION 16:12

*12 And the sixth angel poured out his vial upon the great river Euphrates; and the water thereof was dried up, that the way of the kings of the east might be prepared.(*This is the Ataturk Dam in Turkey that will shut off the flow of water so that the kings of the east can cross over.)

Joel Rosenberg July 15, 2009 ***EUPIIRATES RIVER DRYING UP***: New York Times notes connection to Book of Revelation and the End Times.

The front page of Tuesday morning's New York Times had a stunning headline: ***"Iraq Suffers as the Euphrates River Dwindles."***

From around the world, all of the kings, leaders, generals, armies will gather at Armageddon.

Isa. 66:18 And I, because of what they have planned and done, am about to come and gather the people of all nations and languages, and they will come and see my glory.

Isa 49:2 I will beckon to the nations

Jer. 3:17 all nations will gather in Jerusalem.

Joel . 3: 1 For, behold, in those days, and in that time, when I shall bring again the captives of Judah and Jerusalem, 2. I will also gather all nations, and will bring them down into the valley of Jehoshaphat, and will enter into judgment with them there for my people and for my heritage Israel, whom they have scattered among the nations, and divided up my land. 11 Assemble yourselves, and come, all you nations and gather yourselves together round about: thither cause thy mighty ones to come down, O Lord. 12 Let the nations be roused; let them advance into the Valley of Jehoshaphat, for there I will sit to judge all the nations on every side.

Zephaniah 3:8 Therefore wait upon me, says the Lord, until the day that I rise up to the prey: for my determination is to gather the nations, that I may assemble the kingdoms, to pour upon them mine indignation, even all my fierce anger: for all the earth shall be devoured with the fire of my jealousy. 18 I have decided to assemble the nations.

Isaiah 34:2,3 The Lord is angry with all nations; his wrath is on all their armies. He will totally destroy them; he will give them over to slaughter. Their slain will be thrown out, their dead bodies will stink; the mountains will be soaked with their blood.

Zechariah 14:2 For I will gather all nations against Jerusalem to battle; and the city shall be taken, and the houses plundered, and the women ravished;

and half of the city shall go forth into captivity, and the remnant of the people shall not be cut off from the city. 3 Then shall the Lord go forth and fight against those nations, as when he fought in the day of battle. 4 And his feet shall stand in that day upon the mount of Olives; which is before Jerusalem on the east, and the mount of Olives shall split in two toward the east and toward the west, and there shall be a very great valley; and half of the mountain shall remove toward the north, and half of it toward the south.

Several years ago, a hotel chain was investigating building a hotel on the Mount of Olives and discovered a huge fault line under it. So, of course they didn't build on it.

5 And you shall flee to the valley of the mountains, for the valley of the mountains shall reach unto Azal: yea, ye shall flee, like as ye fled from before the earthquake in the days of Uzziah, king of Judah: and the Lord my God shall come, and all the saints with him. 6 And it shall come to pass in that day, that the light shall not be clear, nor dark: 7 But it shall be one day which shall be known to the Lord, not day, nor night: but it shall come to pass, that at evening time it shall be light.

There will be a world-wide whirlwind. We think we have seen tornadoes and hurricanes, but this will dwarf the worst of them. There will be so many dead that they won't even be buried.

Jeremiah 25:32,33 Thus says the Lord of hosts, Behold, evil shall go forth from nation to nation, and a great whirlwind shall be raised up from the farthest parts of the earth. And the slain of the Lord shall be at that day from end of the earth even unto the other end of the earth: they shall not be lamented, neither gathered, nor buried; they shall be refuse upon the ground.

Daniel 11:40-45

40 And at the time of the end shall the king of the south (Egypt*) push at him:(the Antichrist) and the king of the north* (Russia And Muslim Hordes Of Ezek 38, 39 ?*) shall come against him like a whirlwind, with chariots, and with horsemen, and with many ships; and he shall enter into the countries,* *and shall overflow and pass over. 41 He shall enter also into the glorious land, and many countries shall be overthrown: but these shall escape out of his hand, even Edom, and Moab, and the chief of the children of Ammon* (Jordan.) *42 He shall stretch forth his hand also upon the countries: and the land of Egypt shall not escape. 43 But he shall have power over the treasures of gold and of silver, and over all the precious things of Egypt: and the Libyans and the Ethiopians shall be at his steps. 44 But tidings out of the east* (China *) and out of the north* (Russia, Muslims, Whatever is Left *) shall trouble him: (the* Antichrist*) therefore he shall go forth with great fury to destroy, and utterly to make away many.* (1/3rd Of Earth's Population) *45 And he shall plant the tabernacles of his palace between the seas in the glorious holy mountain; yet he shall come to his end, and none shall help him.*

Revelation 9:17 And thus I saw the horses in the vision, and them that sat on them, having breastplates of fire, and of jacinth, and brimstone: and the heads of the horses were as the heads of lions; and out of their mouths issued fire and smoke and brimstone. (nuclear bombs*?) 18 By these three was the third part of men killed, by the fire, and by the smoke, and by the brimstone, which issued out of their mouths. 19 For their power is in their mouth, and in their tails: for their tails were like unto serpents, and had heads, and with them they do hurt. 20 And the rest of the men which were not killed by these plagues yet repented not of the works of their hands, that they should not worship demons, and idols of gold, and silver, and brass, and stone, and of wood: which neither can see, nor hear, nor walk:*

China's New Silk Road Must Pass Through Middle East

Maurizio Molinari (2014-02-19)

China is talking about a water route between China and the Mediterranean Sea.

Nuclear War: Why nuclear Armageddon is a very real danger

Kyle Mizokami

Zechariah 14:12 This is the plague with which the Lord will strike all the nations that fought against Jerusalem: Their flesh will rot while they are still standing on their feet, their eyes will rot in their sockets, and their tongues will rot in their mouths. 13 On that day people will be stricken bythe Lord with great panic. They will seize each other by the hand and attack one another.

Obadiah 1:15 The day of the Lord is near for all nations. As you (Edom *) have done, it will be done to you; your deeds will return upon your own head. 16 Just as you drank on my holy hill, so all the nations will drink continually; they will drink and drink and be as if they had never been.*

Edom is southeast of the Dead Sea and is the home of Esau's descendants.

Isaiah 13.6 Howl ye; for the day of the LORD is at hand; it shall come as a destruction from the Almighty.7 Therefore shall all hands be faint, and every man's heart shall melt: (from fright) *8 And they shall be afraid: pangs and sorrows shall take hold of them; they shall be in pain as a woman that travails: they shall be amazed at one another; their faces shall be as flames. 9 Behold, the day of the LORD cometh, cruel both with wrath and fierce anger, to lay the land desolate: and he shall destroy the sinners thereof out of it.*

Isaiah 26:21

21 For, behold, the LORD cometh out of his place to punish the inhabitants of the earth for their iniquity: the earth also shall disclose her blood, and shall no more cover her slain.

Revelation 14:18-20

18 And another angel came out from the altar, which had power over fire; and cried with a loud cry to him that had the sharp sickle, saying, Thrust in thy sharp sickle, and gather the clusters of the vine of the earth; for her grapes are fully ripe.

19 And the angel thrust in his sickle into the earth, and gathered the vine of the earth, and cast it into the great winepress of the wrath of God. 20 And the winepress was trodden without the city (Jerusalem,) and blood came out of the winepress, even unto the horse bridles, by the space of a thousand and six hundred furlongs. (200 miles) (the size of Israel.)

Zechariah 14:12 This is the plague with which the Lord will strike all the nations that fought against Jerusalem: Their flesh will rot while they are still standing on their feet, their eyes will rot in their sockets, and their tongues will rot in their mouths. 13 On that day people will be stricken by the Lord with great panic. They will seize each other by the hand and attack one another.

Haggai 2:7 And I will shake all nations, and the desire of all nations shall come: and I will fill the temple with glory, says the Lord of hosts. 21…I will shake the heavens and the earth;

Isaiah 2:12-20 For the day of the Lord shall be upon every one that is proud and lofty…and they shall go into the holes of the rocks…for fear of the Lord……when he arises to shake terribly the earth….in that day a man shall cast his idols of silver, and his idols of gold to go into the clefts of the rocks….

Revelation 6:12 And I beheld when he had opened the sixth seal, and, lo, there was a great earthquake; and the sun became black as sackcloth of hair, and the moon became as blood; and the stars of heaven fell unto the earth, even as a fig tree drops her untimely figs, when she is shaken by a might wind. And the heaven departed as a scroll when it is rolled together; and every mountain and island were moved out of their places.

Isaiah 13:10,13 " For the stars of heaven and the constellations thereof shall not give their light: the sun shall be darkened in his going forth, and the moon shall not cause her light to shine. 13 therefore I will shake the heavens, and the earth shall remove out of her place, in the wrath of the Lord of hosts, and in the day of his fierce anger."

Malachi 4:1 For behold, the day comes, that shall burn as an oven' and all the proud, yes and all that do wickedly, shall be stubble: and the day that comes shall burn them up, says the Lord of hosts, that it shall leave them neither root nor branch. 2 But unto you that fear my name shall the Sun of righteousness arise with healing in his wings: and you shall go forth, and grow up as calves of the stall. 3 And you shall tread down the wicked; for they shall be ashes under the soles of your feet in the day that I shall do this, says the Lord of hosts.

Revelation 9:21 Neither repented they of their murders, nor of their sorceries, nor of their fornication, nor of their thefts.

Isaiah 66: 18 And it shall come to pass, that he who flees from the noise of the fear shall fall into the pit; and he that cometh up out of the midst of the pit shall be taken in the snare: for the windows from on high are open, and the foundations of the earth do shake. 19 The earth is utterly broken down, the earth is clean dissolved, the earth is moved exceedingly. 20 The earth shall reel to and fro like a drunkard, and shall be removed like a cottage; and the transgression thereof shall be heavy upon it; and it shall fall, and not rise again. 21 And it shall come to pass in that day, that the LORD shall punish the host of the high ones that are on high, (Satan's demons in the heavens) *and the kings of the earth upon the earth. 22 And they shall be gathered together, as prisoners are gathered in the pit, and shall be shut up in the prison, and after many days shall they be visited. 23 Then the moon shall be confounded, and the sun ashamed, when the LORD of hosts shall reign in mount Zion, and in Jerusalem, and before his ancients gloriously.*

What about all of the people who have been persecuted and killed in the name of Jesus during the tribulation? Does the Bible tell us about them?

Revelation 7: 9 After this I beheld, and, lo, a great multitude, which no man could number, of all nations, and kindreds, and people, and languages, stood before the throne, and before the Lamb, clothed with white robes, and palm branches in their hands; 10 And cried with a loud voice saying, Salvation to our God which sits upon the throne, and to the Lamb. 11 And all the angels stood round about the throne, and about the elders and the four living creatures, and fell before the throne on their faces, and worshiped God, 12 Saying Amen: Blessing, and glory, and wisdom, and thanksgiving, and honor, and power, and might, be unto our God forever and ever. Amen. 13 And one of the elders answered, saying to me, Who are these which are arrayed in white robes? And where did they come from? 14 And I said to him, Sir, you know. And he said to me, These are they which came out of great tribulation, and have washed their robes, and made them white in the blood of the Lamb.

CHAPTER 22

The Return of Christ

Then, after the tribulation, the heavens are going to be shaken.

Matt. 24:29 "Immediately after the tribulation of those days shall the sun be darkened, and the moon shall not give her light, and the stars shall fall from heaven, and the powers of the heavens shall be shaken.

Isaiah 34:4 All the stars in the sky will be dissolved, and the heavens rolled up like a scroll; all the starry host will fall, like withered leaves from the vine, like shriveled figs from the fig tree.

Isaiah 13:12 Therefore I will make the heavens tremble; and the earth will shake from its place at the wrath of the Lord Almighty, in the day of his burning anger.

There will be no light from the sun and moon; the stars will disappear.

Joel 3:15, 16 "The sun and the moon shall be darkened, and the stars shall withdraw their shining. The Lord also shall roar out of Zion, and utter his voice from Jerusalem; and the heavens and the earth shall shake."

Isaiah 13:10,13 " For the stars of heaven and the constellations thereof shall not give their light: the sun shall be darkened in his going forth, and the moon shall not cause her light to shine. 13 therefore I will shake the heavens, and the earth shall remove out of her place, in the wrath of the Lord of hosts, and in the day of his fierce anger."

Matt. 24:30 "And then shall appear the sign of the Son of man in heaven: and then shall all the tribes of the earth mourn, and they shall see the Son of man coming in the clouds of heaven with power and great glory..31 And he shall send his angels with a great sound of a trumpet, and they shall gather together his elect from the four winds, from one end of heaven to the other"

Revelation 19:11 "I saw heaven standing open and there before me was a white horse, whose rider is called Faithful and True. With justice he judges and wages war. 12 His eyes are like blazing fire, and on his head are many crowns. He has a name written on him that no one knows but he himself. 13 He is dressed in a robe dipped in blood, and his name is the Word of God. 14 The armies of heaven were following him, riding on white horses and dressed in fine linen, white and clean.......16 On his robe and on his thigh he has this name written: King of Kings and Lord of Lords."

Psalm 149 . .to execute vengeance..this honor have all his saints... We, the saints will be coming back with Him to execute vengeance on those fighting against Him.

Micah 1:3 "For, behold, the Lord comes forth out of his place, and will come down, and tread upon the high places of the earth. 4 And the mountains shall melt under him, and the valleys shall split, as wax before the fire, and as the waters that are poured down a steep place."

Revelation 11:*15 "The seventh angel sounded his trumpet, and there were loud voices in heaven which said: 'The kingdom of the world has become the kingdom of our Lord and of his Messiah, and he will reign forever and ever.'"*

The Son of man will come down from heaven and send his angels to gather his elect. This finishes the last of the Trumpet Judgments. The Mystery is finished and the temple in heaven is opened, celebrating the kingdom of God and his Messiah to reign forever. It is accompanied by lightning, thunder, an earthquake and a severe hailstorm.

Jesus, the Word, and His army defeat the Antichrist and the world's armies. The Antichrist and the False Prophet are thrown into the Lake of Fire.

Revelation 19:19 "Then I saw the beast and the kings of the earth and their armies gathered together to wage war against the rider on the horse and his army. 20 But the beast was captured, and with it the false prophet who had performed the signs on its behalf. With these signs he had deluded those who had received the mark of the beast and worshiped its image. The two of them were thrown alive into the fiery lake of burning sulfur. 21 The rest were killed with the sword coming out of the mouth of the rider on the horse."

Satan is bound in the bottomless pit for a thousand years. Those who are saved will reign with Christ for a thousand years. After that Satan will be released once more, to gather again the nations which will be devoured by fire from heaven. He will then be thrown into the lake of fire with the beast and the false prophet and tormented forever.

CHAPTER 23

The Marriage Supper of the Lamb

While the rest of the world is enduring the tribulation, the Church will be enjoying the Marriage Supper as the Bride of Christ. But this is the part that keeps me awake at night: Jesus told a parable about a wedding party waiting for the groom to come. The groom couldn't go for his bride until his Father told him that the new home that he was preparing was perfectly ready. The wedding party had come to wait for the Bridegroom and some were ready with extra oil for their lamps to light the way when the Bridegroom came, while others ran out of oil. While going to buy oil for their lamps, the unprepared virgins missed the sudden arrival of the bridegroom and the door was shut so that they could not go in to the wedding.

Matthew 25: 10 But while they (the ones who were not ready,) *were on their way to buy the oil* (for their lamps,) *the bridegroom* (Jesus,*) arrived. The virgins (*the church,) *who were ready went in with him to the wedding banquet. And the door was shut.*

Is the church ready? Are we ready? Which ones will be taken? Which ones will be left? If the oil signifies the Holy Spirit who gives light to the church so that the church can light up the darkness around us, are there some in the church who are waiting without the Holy Spirit?

CHAPTER 24

Heaven on Earth - The Millennium

Revelation 21 and 22 tells us about a new heaven, a new earth and a new Jerusalem , which is the home of the Bride of Christ. We will have the river of life flowing around us and the tree of life yielding fruit every month.

Revelation 21:1-4 Then I saw a new heaven and a new earth, for the first heaven and the first earth had passed away, and there was no longer any sea. I saw the Holy City, the new Jerusalem, coming down out of heaven from God, prepared as a bride beautifully dressed for her husband. And I heard a loud voice from the throne saying, "Look! God's dwelling place is now among the people, and he will dwell with them. They will be his people, and God himself will be with them and be their God. He will wipe every tear from their eyes. There will be no more death or mourning or crying or pain, for the old order of things has passed away.

Revelation 22: 1 "Then the angel showed me the river of the water of life, as clear as crystal, flowing from the throne of God and of the Lamb 2. ......On each side of the river stood the tree of life, bearing twelve crops of fruit, yielding its fruit every month."

QUESTIONS ABOUT HEAVEN:

Question: How many heavens are there?

Deuteronomy 10:14 To the Lord your God belong the heavens, even the highest heavens, the earth and everything in it.

Corinthians 12:2 I know a man in Christ…whether in the body…or out of the body, I cannot tell: such a one caught up to the third heaven."

Question: Has God dwelt on earth? Will He in the future?

Jeremiah 23:24 Who can hide in secret places so that I cannot see them? declares the Lord. Do not I fill heaven and earth?

1 Kings 8:27 But will God really dwell on earth? The heavens, even the highest heaven, cannot contain you. How much less this temple I have built!

Job 22:12 Is not God in the heights of heaven? And see how lofty are the highest stars!

Psalm 89:6 For who in the skies above can compare with the Lord? Who is like the Lord among the heavenly beings? 7 In the council of the holy ones God is greatly feared; he is more awesome than all who surround him.

Question: Who has the title deed to earth?

Psalm 115:16 The highest heavens belong to the Lord, but the earth he has given to mankind.

Question: Will there be, on this renovated earth, people who marry and have families?

Isaiah 65:17 See, I will create new heavens and a new earth. The former things will not be remembered, nor will they come to mind. 18 But be glad and rejoice forever in what I will create, for I will create Jerusalem to be a delight and its people a joy. 19 I will rejoice over Jerusalem and take delight in my people; the sound of weeping and of crying will be heard in it no more. 20 Never again will there be in it an infant who lives but a few days, or an old man who does not live out his years; the one who dies at a hundred will be thought a mere child; the one who fails to reach a hundred will be considered accursed.

21 They will build houses and dwell in them; they will plant vineyards and eat their fruit. No longer will they build houses and others live in them, or plant and others eat. For as the days of a tree, so will be the days of my people; my chosen ones will long enjoy the work of their hands. They will not labor in vain, nor will they bear children doomed to misfortune; for they will be a people blessed by the Lord, they and their descendants with them, 24 Before they call I will answer; while they are still speaking I will hear. The wolf and the lamb will feed together, and the lion will eat straw like the ox, and dust will be the serpent's food. They will neither harm nor destroy on all my holy mountain, says the Lord.

Question: If there is no pain and sadness, how will people die? What about marriage if there are children being born? Are these people who lived through the tribulation?

Ezekiel 1: Vision of heaven

Daniel 7:13 In my vision at night I looked, and there before me was one like a son of man, coming with the clouds of heaven. He approached the Ancient of Days and was led into his presence. He was given authority, glory and sovereign power; all nations and peoples of every language worshiped him. His dominion is an everlasting dominion that will not pass away, and his kingdom is one that will never be destroyed.

Question: Who is the Ancient of Days? Why is He called that?

Haggai 2:6 This is what the Lord Almighty says: In a little while I will once more shake the heavens and the earth, the sea, and the dry land. I will shake all nations, and what is desired by all nations will come, and I will fill this house with glory, says the Lord Almighty.

Question: What is desired of all nations?

Hebrews 12:22 But you have come to Mount Zion, to the city of the living God, the heavenly Jerusalem. You have come to thousands upon thousands of angels in joyful assembly, 23 to the church of the firstborn, whose names are written in heaven. You have come to God, the Judge of all, to the spirits of the righteous made perfect, to Jesus the mediator of a new covenant, and to the sprinkled blood that speaks a better word than the blood of Abel.

Question: Is there a Mount Zion in heaven? Is it another Jerusalem?

Question: What is the church of the firstborn?

Revelation 1 – DESCRIPTION OF HEAVEN

Rev. 21:1 And I saw a new heaven and a new earth: for the first heaven and the first earth were passed away; and there was no more sea.

Question: Why no more sea? What does this mean?

Revelation 21:2 And I John saw the holy city, new Jerusalem, coming down from God out of heaven, prepared as a bride adorned for her husband. 3 And I heard a great voice out of heaven saying, Behold, the tabernacle of God is with men, and he will dwell with them, and they shall be his people, and God himself shall be with them, and be their God.

Question: What happens in Heaven? Who is there?

Revelation 21:4 And God shall wipe away all tears from their eyes; and there shall be no more death, neither sorrow, nor crying, neither shall there be any more pain: for the former things are passed away. 5 And he that sat upon the throne said, Behold, I make all things new. And he said unto me, Write: for these words are true and faithful. 6 And he said to me, It is done. I am Alpha and Omega, the beginning and the end. I will give to him that is thirsty of the fountain of the water of life freely. 7 He that overcomes shall inherit all things; and I will be his God, and he shall be my son.

Question: What does it take to overcome?

1 John 5:4 "For whosever is born of God overcomes the world: and this is the victory that overcomes the world, even our faith. 5 Who is he that overcomes the world, but he that believes that Jesus is the Son of God."

Revelation 21:7 Those who are victorious will inherit all this, and I will be their God and they will be my children. 8 But the cowardly, the unbelieving, the vile, the murderers, the sexually immoral, those who practice magic arts, the idolaters and all liars – they will be consigned to the fiery lake of burning sulfur. This is the second death."

Question: Will God really let people burn forever?

Revelation 14:11 And the smoke of their torment ascends up forever and ever: and they have no rest day nor night, who worship the beast and his image, and whoever receives the mark of his name.

Revelation 21:9 And there came to me one of the seven angels which had the seven bowls full of the seven last plagues, and talked with me, saying, Come hither, I will show you the bride, the Lamb's wife.

Question: Who is the Lamb? Who is the Lamb's wife?

Revelation 21:10 And he carried me away in the Spirit to a great and high mountain, and showed me that great city, the holy Jerusalem, descending out of heaven from God, 11 having the glory of God: and her light was like a stone most precious, even like a jasper stone, clear as crystal; 12 And had a wall great and high, and had twelve gates, and at the gates twelve angels, and names written on it, which are twelve tribes of the children of Israel: 13 And on the east three gates; on the north three gates; on the south three gates; and on the west three gates.

Question: Why are there twelve gates?

Revelation 21:14 And the wall of the city had twelve foundations, and in them the names of the twelve apostles of the Lamb. 15 And he that talked with me had a golden reed to measure the city, and the gates thereof, and the wall thereof. 16 And the city is laid out as a square, and the length is as large as the breadth: and he measured the city with the reed, twelve thousand furlongs. The length and the breadth and the height of it are equal.

Question: How big is that?

And he measured the wall thereof, a hundred and forty and four cubits, according to the measure of a man, that is, of the angel.

And the construction of the wall of it was of jasper: and the city was pure gold, like clear glass.

Question: What does pure gold look like?

And the foundations of the wall of the city were adorned with all manner of precious stones. The first foundation was jasper; the second, sapphire; the third, a chalcedony; the fourth, and emerald; the fifth, sardonyx; the sixth, sardius; the seventh, chrysolite; the eighth, beryl; the ninth, a topaz; the tenth, a chrysoprasus; the eleventh, a jacinth, the twelfth, an amethyst.

And the twelve gates were twelve pearls; every individual gate was of one pearl: and the street of the city was pure gold, as it were transparent glass.

And I saw no temple therein: for the Lord God Almighty and the Lamb are the temple of it.

Question: Are God and the Lamb going to reside there? How can that be?

And the city had no need of the sun, neither of the moon, to shine in it: for the glory of God did lighten it, and the Lamb is the light thereof.

And the nations of them which are saved shall walk in the light of it: and the kings of the earth do bring their glory and honor into it.

Question: Are there nations of saved people on the renovated earth?

And the gates of it shall not be shut at all by day: for there shall be no night there.

And they shall bring the glory and honor of the nations into it.

And there shall in no wise enter into it anything that defiles, neither whatsoever causes an abomination, or makes a lie: but they which are written in the Lamb's book of life.

Question: Are there nations of unsaved people?

River of Life Flows from the Throne of God and the Lamb

Rev. 22: " And he showed me a pure river of water of life, clear as crystal, proceeding out of the throne of God and of the Lamb. In the middle of the street, and on either side of the river, was the tree of life, which bare twelve manner of fruits, and yielded her fruit every month: and the leaves of the tree were for the healing of the nations."

Question: What is this water of life?

Psalm 46:4 "There is a river, the streams whereof shall make glad the city of God, the holy place of the dwelling places of the Most High God."

Question: Is this in Heaven or on earth?

Joel 3:18 "And it shall come to pass in that day, that the mountains shall drop down new wine, and the hills shall flow with milk, and all the rivers of Judah shall flow with waters, and a fountain shall come forth of the house of the Lord, and shall water the valley of Acacias."

Question: Is this literally wine and milk? What does it mean?

Ezekiel 47 "it was a river that I could not cross....behold, at the bank of the river were very many trees on the one side and on the other.....they shall be healed...by the river upon the bank thereof, ...shall grow all trees for food, whose leaf shall not wither, neither shall the fruit thereof fail: it shall bring forth new fruit every month....and the fruit shall be for food and the leaf thereof for medicine."

Question: Are these two scriptures talking about the same things?

Revelation 22:17 And the Spirit and the bride say come. And let him that hear say, Come. And whosoever desires, let him take the water of life freely.

The King and His Kingdom

Daniel 2:44 "And in the days of these kings shall the God of heaven set up a kingdom, which shall never be destroyed: and the kingdom shall not be left to other people, but it shall break in pieces and consume all these kingdoms, and it shall stand forever."

Habakkuk 2:14 "The earth shall be filled with the knowledge of the glory of the Lord, as the waters cover the sea.

Revelation 20: 6 Blessed and holy is he that has part in the first resurrection: on such the second death has no power, but they shall be priests of God and of Christ, and shall reign with him a thousand years.

Obadiah 1: 17 But upon mount Zion shall be salvation, and it shall be holy; and the house of Jacob shall possess their possessions.

Isa. 2:2 And it shall come to pass in the last days, that the mountain of the Lord's house shall be established in the top of the mountains, and shall be exalted above the hills; and all nations shall flow unto it.

3 And many people shall go and say, Come and let us go up to the mountain of the Lord, to the house of the God of Jacob; and he will teach us of his ways, and we will walk in his paths: for out of Zion shall go forth the law, and the word of the Lord from Jerusalem.

4 And he shall judge among the nations, and shall rebuke many people: and they shall beat their swords into plowshares, and their spears into pruning hooks: nation shall not lift up sword against nation, neither shall they learn war any more.

Micah says almost the same thing.

Micah 4:1 But in the last days it shall come to pass, that the mountain of the house of the Lord shall be established in the top of the mountains, and it shall be exalted above the hills; and people shall flow unto it. 2.And many nations shall come, and say, Come, and let us go up to the mountain of the Lord, and to the house of the God of Jacob; and he will teach us of his ways, and we will walk in his paths: for the law shall go forth of Zion, and the word of the Lord from Jerusalem. 3. And he shall judge among many people, and rebuke strong nations afar off; and they shall beat their swords into plowshares, and their spears into pruning hooks: nation shall not lift up a sword against nation, neither shall they learn war any more. 4. But they shall sit every man under his vine and under his fig tree; and none shall make them afraid: for the mouth of the Lord of hosts has spoken it. 5. For all people will walk everyone in the name of his god, and we will walk in the name of the Lord our God forever and ever.

Zech. 14:2 And it shall be in that day, that living waters shall go out from Jerusalem; half of them toward the Dead sea, and half of them toward the Mediterranean sea: in summer and in winter shall it be 3 And the Lord shall be king over all the earth: in that day shall there be one Lord, and his name one. 4 All the land shall be turned into a plain from Geba to Rimmon south of Jerusalem: and Jerusalem shall be lifted up and inhabited in her place, from Benjamin's gate unto the place of the first gate, unto the corner gate, and from the tower of Hananeel unto the king's winepresses. 5 And men shall dwell in it, and there shall be no more utter destruction; but Jerusalem shall be safely inhabited. 6 And it shall come to pass, that every one that is left of all the nations which came against Jerusalem shall even go up from year to year to worship the King, the Lord of hosts, and to keep the feast of tabernacles. 7 And it shall be, that whoso will not come up of all the families of the earth to Jerusalem to worship the King, the Lord of hosts, even upon them shall be no rain.

Zephaniah 3:9 For then I will restore to the people a pure language, that they may all call upon the name of the Lord, to serve him with one accord.

Haggai 2:9 The glory of the temple shall be greater than of the former, says the Lord of hosts: and in this place will I give peace, says the Lord of hosts.

CHAPTER 25

The Final Battle, Judgment and Eternity

After the Millennium:

Satan will be released after a thousand years and will gather the nations again to battle. Fire will come down from heaven and devour them. The devil will be cast into the lake of fire.

Revelation 20:7 And when the thousand years are completed, Satan shall be released out of his prison, 8 and shall go out to deceive the nations which are in the four quarters of the earth, God and Magog, to gather them together to battle: the number of whom is as the sand of the sea. 9. And they went up on the breadth of the earth, and surrounded the camp of the saints about, and the beloved city: and fire came down from God out of heaven, and devoured them.

There will be a Great White Throne Judgment Seat and those who are not found in the book of life will be cast into the lake of fire.

The Judgment Seat

Daniel 7:9-10 "As I looked, thrones were set in place and the Ancient of Days took his seat. His clothing was as white as snow; the hair of his head was white like wool. His throne was flaming with fire, and its wheels were all ablaze. A river of fire was flowing coming out from before him. Thousands upon thousands attended him; ten thousand times stood before him. The court was seated, and the books were opened. I kept looking until the beast was slain and its body destroyed and thrown into the blazing fire. (The other beasts had been stripped of their authority, but were allowed to live for a period of time. In my vision at night I looked, and there before me was one like a son of man, coming with the clouds of heaven. He approached the Ancient of Days and was led into his presence. He was given authority, glory and sovereign power; all nations and peoples of every language worshiped him. His dominion is an everlasting dominion that will not pass away, and his kingdom is one that will never be destroyed.

Revelation 20:11 And I saw a great white throne, and him that sat on it, from whose face the earth and the heaven fled away; and there was found no place for them. 12 And I saw the dead, small and great, stand before God; and the books were opened: and another book was opened, which is the book of life: and the dead were judged out of those things which were written in the books, according to their works. 13 And the sea gave up the dead which were in it; and death and hades delivered up the dead which were in them: and they were judged every man according to their works. 14 And death and hades were cast into the lake of fire. This is the second death. 15 And whoever was not found written in the book of life was cast into the lake of fire.

CHAPTER 26

Here I Come – Ready or Not!

Thessalonians 2:1-3 " Concerning the coming of our Lord Jesus Christ and our being gathered to him, we ask you, brothers and sisters, not to become easily unsettled or alarmed by the teaching allegedly from us ....asserting that the day of the Lord has already come. Don't' let anyone deceive you in any way, for that day will not come until the rebellion occurs and the man of lawlessness is revealed."

God's time table is not like ours. He counts thousands of years as days:

"But, beloved, be not ignorant of this one thing, that one day is with the Lord as a thousand years, and a thousand years as one day." 2 Peter 3:8

Realizing that it has been over two thousand years since Christ died for us, then we are on the third year of the end of days.

Hosea 6:1 Come, and let us return to the Lord: for he has torn and he will heal us; he has stricken, and he will bandage us up. 2 After two days he will revive us: in the third day, he will raise us up, and we shall live in his sight.

Matthew 25, right after Jesus answers the disciples questions about when he will return, he tells the parable of foolish virgins, who went to meet the bridegroom, took lamps without extra oil and went to sleep. At midnight, there was a shout, "The Bridegroom is coming."

The churches are the virgins, some foolish and some wise, some ready and some not ready for the arrival of the Bridegroom, Jesus. Some have oil in their lamps, ready, but others have not kept their lamps burning. Those without the oil of the Spirit will search everywhere to buy oil but it will be too late, they will try to get in, but the door will be shut and Jesus, the Bridegroom will reply, " I never knew you. When I stood at your closed door knocking, you would not let me in so I never had fellowship and we never knew each other. You were sleeping and you did not care about the oil that would light your way and then you got frantic and it was too dark to find the oil."

Peter 2:20 For if after they have escaped the pollutions of the world through the knowledge of the Lord and Savior Jesus Christ, they are again entangled therein, and overcome, the latter end is worse with them than the beginning. 21 For it had been better for them not to have known the way of righteousness, than after they have known it, to turn from the holy commandment delivered to them.

THE SEVEN CHURCHES: Question: Who are the over-comers? Revelation talks about seven types of over-comers in Revelation 2-3.

When we start talking about the seven churches, remember that these are not only seven real churches in Asia at the time, but they also represent seven church ages. More importantly, I think they represent seven kinds of Christians.

1. Ephesus – *"These are the words of him who holds the seven stars in his right hand and walks among the seven golden lamp stands. I know your deeds, your hard work and your perseverance. I know that you cannot tolerate wicked people, that you have tested those who claim to be apostles but are not, and have found them false. You have persevered and have endured hardships for my name, and have not grown weary."*

"Yet I hold this against you: You have forsaken the love you had at first. Consider how far you have fallen! Repent! And do the things you did at first. If you do not repent, I will come to you and remove your lamp stand from its place. But you have this in your favor: You hate the practices of the Nicolaitans, which I also hate."

"Whoever has ears, let them hear what the Spirit says to the churches. To the one who is victorious, I will give the right to eat from the tree of life, which is in the paradise of God."

They worked and labored and hated those who were evil and persevered without fainting. But they had left their first love, Jesus. *Revelation 2:4 " I hold this against you: you have left your first love."*

They were working without loving Jesus, but they hated the Nicolaitans who believed that liberty in Christ meant that you could engage in any licentiousness. Some are going to be removed from their place because they left their first love and some because they thought their freedom in Christ allowed them to become morally unrestrained.

Isaiah 66:4b "For when I called, no one answered; when I spoke, no one listened. They did evil in my sight and chose what displeases me." Unless they repent and come back to their first love, they will be removed. ***If they overcome***, they will eat of the tree of life.

2. Smyrna – *"These are the words of him who is the First and the Last, who died and came to life again. I know your afflictions and your poverty—yet you are rich! I know about the slander of those who say they are Jews and are not, but are a synagogue of Satan. Do not be afraid of what you are about to suffer. I tell you, the devil will put some of you in prison, to test you, and you will suffer persecution for ten days. Be faithful, even to the point of death, and I will give you life as your victor's crown."*

"Whoever has ears, let them hear what the Spirit says to the churches. The one who is victorious will not be hurt at all by the second death."

They had worked and gone through persecution and poverty, but they were faithful to the point of death.

Some will go through persecution to be tested by Satan. ***If they continue to overcome***, they will not be hurt by the second death.

3. Pergamos – *"These are the words of him who has the sharp, double-edged sword. I know where you live—where Satan has his throne. Yet you remain true to my name. You did not renounce your faith in me, not even in the days of Antipas, my faithful witness, who was put to death in your city—where Satan lives."*

"Nevertheless, I have a few things against you: There are some among you who hold to the teaching of Balaam, who taught Balak to entice the Israelites to sin so that they ate food sacrificed to idols and committed sexual immorality. Likewise, you also have those who hold to the teaching of the Nicolaitans. Repent therefore! Otherwise, I will soon come to you and will fight against them with the sword of my mouth."

"Whoever has ears, let them hear what the Spirit says to the churches. To the one who is victorious, I will give some of the hidden manna. I will also give that person a white stone with a new name written on it, known only to the one who receives it"

They were living right in the middle of where Satan was seated, while still holding onto Jesus' name and not denying the faith, but they compromised with the pagans around them by sacrificing to idols and committing fornication, (sexual immorality.) Jesus will fight them with the sword of His Word and will destroy them because they have not believed in the priesthood and salvation of Jesus. Some will fight Him because they indulged in the sin of the world. ***If they overcome***, Jesus will give them hidden manna and a white stone with a new name written on it.

4. Thyatira – *"These are the words of the Son of God, whose eyes are like blazing fire and whose feet are like burnished bronze. I know your deeds, your love and faith, your service and perseverance, and that you are now doing more than you did at first."*

"Nevertheless, I have this against you: You tolerate that woman Jezebel, who calls herself a prophet. By her teaching she misleads my servants into sexual immorality and the eating of food sacrificed to idols. I have given her time to repent of her immorality, but she is unwilling. So I will cast her on a

bed of suffering and I will make those who commit adultery with her suffer intensely, unless they repent of her ways. I will strike her children dead. Then all the churches will know that I am he who searches hearts and minds, and I will repay each of you according to your deeds."

"Now I say to the rest of you in Thyatira, to you who do not hold to her teaching and have not learned Satan's so-called deep secrets, 'I will not impose any other burden on you, except to hold on to what you have until I come."

"To the one who is victorious and does my will to the end, I will give authority over the nations—that one will rule them with an iron scepter and will dash them to pieces like pottery—just as I have received authority from my Father. I will also give that one the morning star. Whoever has ears, let them hear what the Spirit says to the churches."

They were involved in good works, charity, service, faith and had patience, but allowed the Jezebel spirit into their lives which seduced them to commit sexual immorality and to sacrifice to idols. They that commit adultery with that spirit will be cast into great tribulation, unless they repent. ***To those who overcome,*** Jesus will give power over the nations, to rule over them. He will also give them the morning star. Jesus searches hearts and minds.

5. Sardis –*"These are the words of him who holds the seven spirits of and the seven stars. I know your deeds; you have a reputation of being alive, but you are dead. Wake up! Strengthen what remains and is about to die, for I have found your deeds unfinished in the sight of my God. Remember, therefore, what you have received and heard; hold it fast, and repent. But if you do not wake up, I will come like a thief, and you will not know at what time I will come to you."*

"Yet you have a few people in Sardis who have not soiled their clothes. They will walk with me, dressed in white, for they are worthy. The one who is victorious, will, like them, be dressed in white. I will never blot out the name of that person from the book of life, but will acknowledge that name before

my Father and his angels. Whoever has ears, let them hear what the Spirit says to the churches."

Jesus said they had a name of being alive but they were dead. "*Repent or I will come on you as a thief." **If they overcome***, they will be clothed in a white garment, and their names will not be blotted out of the book of life. Did you know your name can be blotted out of the book of life?

Here lies Sardis, dead. They must wake up. Jesus will catch them like a thief, unprepared, unsaved, already dead like the rest of the world but thinking themselves saved. They will go through the tribulation.

6. Philadelphia – "*These are the words of him who is holy and true, who holds the key of David. What he opens no one can shut, and what he shuts no one can open. I know your deeds. See, I have placed before you an open door that no one can shut. I know that you have little strength, yet you have kept my word and have not denied my name. I will make those who are of the synagogue of Satan, who claim to be Jews though they are not, but are liars—I will make them come and fall down at your feet and acknowledge that I have loved you. Since you have kept my command to endure patiently, I will also keep you from the hour of trial that is going to come on the whole word to test the inhabitants of the earth."*

"I am coming soon. Hold on to what you have, so that no one will take your crown. The one who is victorious I will make a pillar in the temple of my God. Never again will they leave it. I will write on them the name of my God and the name of the city of my God, the new Jerusalem, which is coming down out of heaven from my God; and I will also write on them my new name. Whoever has ears, let them hear what the Spirit says to the churches."

This church has an open door and because they let Jesus come in, they will go in the door at the rapture. "You have kept my word. Some of you, because you have kept my command to endure patiently, I will keep you from the hour of trial that will come upon the whole world." ***He who overcomes***, will be in the presence of God and will be given Jesus' new name.

7. Laodicea – "*These are the words of the Amen, the faithful and true witness, the ruler of God's creation. I know your deeds, that you are neither cold nor hot. I wish you were either one or the other! So, because you are lukewarm—neither hot nor cold—I am about to spit you out of my mouth. You say, I am rich; I have acquired wealth and do not need a thing. But you do not realize that you are wretched, pitiful, poor, blind, and naked. I counsel you to buy from me gold refined in the fire, so you can become rich; and white clothes to wear, so you can cover your shameful nakedness; and salve to put on your eyes, so you can see.*"

"*Those whom I love I rebuke and discipline. So be earnest and repent. Her I am! I stand at the door and knock. If anyone hears my voice and opens the door, I will come in and eat with that person, and they with me.*"

"*To the one who is victorious, I will give the right to sit with me on my throne just as I was victorious, and sat down with my Father on his throne. Whoever has ears, let them hear what the Spirit says to the churches.*"

They were lukewarm and it made Jesus sick. They were rich in goods but poor in spirit. Ouch! The church of Laodicea was lukewarm, blind, thinking they were rich but they were poor, naked, and blind. They must buy gold tried in fire, white garments, eye salve and open the door to Jesus. (Complacent, satisfied, are these Christians who do not know the power of the Holy Spirit?)

Romans 12:21 Be not overcome of evil, but overcome evil with good.

1 John 5:4 For whatever is born of God overcomes the world: and this is the victory that overcomes the world, even our faith. 5 Who is he that overcomes the world, but he that believes that Jesus is the Son of God.

John 16:33 "These things I have spoken to you, that in me you might have peace. In the world you shall have tribulation: but be of good cheer; I have overcome the world."

1 Thessalonians 5:1-10 "Now, brothers and sisters, about times and dates we do not need to write to you, for you know very well that the day of the

Lord will come like a thief in the night. While people are saying, 'Peace and safety,' destruction will come on them suddenly, as labor pains on a pregnant woman, and they will not escape."

"But you, brothers and sisters, are not in darkness so that this day should surprise you like a thief. You are all children of the light and children of the day. We do not belong to the night or to the darkness.

So then, let us not be like others, who are asleep, but let us be awake and sober. For those who sleep, sleep at night, and those who get drunk, get drunk at night. But since we belong to the day, let us be sober, putting on faith and love as a breastplate, and the hope of salvation as a helmet. For God did not appoint us to suffer wrath but to receive salvation through our Lord Jesus Christ. He died for us so that, whether we are awake or asleep, we may live together with him."

Revelation 1:3 Blessed is he that reads and they that hear the words of this prophecy, and keep those things which are written there: ***for the time is at hand.***